*Igniting the
Moral Courage
Of America*

Igniting the Moral Courage Of America

Six Ways You Can Inspire People To Live With Integrity

Dean Kilmer

MORAL COURAGE
PUBLICATIONS
716 McMurry
Waxahachie, TX 75165
website: www.moralcourage.net
email: dean@moralcourage.net

Copyright © 2006
Dean Kilmer

ISBN: 0-9760327-8-3

Unless otherwise noted, all Scriptures are taken from the HOLY BIBLE, NEW INTERNATIONAL VERSION ®, Copyright © 1973, 1978, 1984 by International Bible Society. Used by permission of Zondervan. All rights reserved.

Dedication

To my grandchildren

Clay, McKenzie, and Connor

and
to those who may follow
with the constant prayer
that they will have a great faith in God
and that their generation will help
our country to return to God.

Contents

Chapter 1: Examining America's Moral Decline	1
Step One: Energizing People of Integrity	**15**
Chapter 2: The Kidnapping of Our Integrity!	17
Chapter 3: Energizing People of Integrity	29
Step Two: Restoring Our Families	**49**
Chapter 4: Four Daggers in the Heart Of the American Family	51
Chapter 5: Rebuilding the Family Of the American Dream	71
Step Three: Igniting Moral Courage	**85**
Chapter 6: The Collapse of Our Moral Strength	87
Chapter 7: Inspiring Americans to Live With Moral Courage	95
Step Four: Reclaiming Our Schools	**121**
Chapter 8: How Could This Happen In Our Schools?	123
Chapter 9: Dynamic Character Development In Our Schools	133
Step Five: Rebuilding the Foundation	**143**
Chapter 10: Why We Are Living on Quicksand?	145
Chapter 11: The Foundation: Absolute Truth, Coupled with Amazing Grace	153
Step Six: Allowing God to Empower You	**167**
Chapter 12: You Are the Answer for America!	169
Bibliography	179

Acknowledgments

Special thanks are due to
Sherry Welch, Charlotte Loyd, and
my wife, Karen,
for their help in proofreading this book,
and to
Andy Brazil for the cover design.

I would like to thank the staff at
Resource Publications, Searcy, Arkansas,
for their excellent work
in preparing the book.

A Note to Readers

The stories in this book
are true;
however, many of the names
have been changed.

1
Examining America's Moral Decline

Igniting America's moral courage sounds like an incredibly daunting task, doesn't it? Before you slough it off as too big a job, read the next few pages! As we approach the mission of improving our nation's moral standards, you may ask yourself, "How can *I* affect the future of the whole nation?" The answer, of course, is *you* can't! However, if you will allow God to work in you, He not only will control your heart, but He will expand your influence in ways that you could never imagine.

It surprises people when I tell them that many of my heroes are elderly widows, some of whom have had a great impact on my life and the lives of other people. On a warm August day, I stopped to talk with ninety-two-year-old Durcie Turner as she mowed the lawn at her little house. It was always fun to stop by her house because she had the warmest toothless smile I've ever seen, and the vegetables from her garden were some of the best in town. This pleasant, cheerful, little lady, who had been fighting cancer for almost six years, never complained about her health problems. Her contagiously positive attitude had a great impact on my life.

Not long after her ninety-third birthday, the cancer got the best of Durcie, and she was forced into the hospital. Now if you can get the picture, this was an eighty-six-pound, ninety-three-year-old lady, who was in pain every minute of her life, lying alone in the hospital, waiting to die. She had every reason to be bitter and unhappy. However, she had such a wonderful attitude that I would wait until I was a little down to go see her because she always picked me up with her cheerful spirit. The first time I visited Durcie, I took my Bible and read from John 1. Her response was, "Dean, that's my favorite passage of Scripture." The second time I visited her, the passage was John 2. She responded, "That's my favorite passage of Scripture." The next visit was John 3, and of course Durcie exclaimed, "That's my favorite passage of Scripture." Durcie loved God's Word. She loved life, and she loved people. The only thing Durcie didn't like was nursing homes. She had heard some stories about nursing homes that scared her, so her goal was either to go home and finish harvesting her garden or to go home and be with the Lord in heaven. The only thing she didn't want was to be placed in a nursing home.

Things got worse for Durcie as the doctors realized there was nothing they could do for her in the hospital and determined that she needed to go to a nursing home. She now weighed eighty-four pounds, couldn't get out of bed, was in constant pain, and was in the one place in the world she didn't want to be. I must admit that I hesitated before going to see her for the first time in that place. I remember the sterile appearance, the nursing home smell, and the big metal door; this just didn't seem to be the right place for this sweet, little, elderly lady. After a little hesitation, I opened the door and walked in, and from the second bed I heard an excited voice saying, "Dean, come over here. I've got something to tell you." I walked to her bedside, looked at that wonderful toothless smile, and asked, "Durcie, what are you so excited about?" She pointed to the bed next to hers and remarked, "That's Jo Ann, and that's the reason God put me here!" What an incredible spirit! She went on to explain that Jo Ann had suffered a stroke that caused her to lose the use of her body, except for one arm and one leg. Durcie explained that sometimes Jo Ann would kick off her covers with that one leg and would then get cold. At other times, when she was hurting, she would raise her arm so Durcie would know that she was in pain. Although Durcie couldn't get out of bed to help her, she could hit the call button to let the nurses know that Jo Ann needed help. It was now her mission in life to care for Jo Ann. With that mission and a call button, she drove the nurses crazy!

Durcie had such an impact on people that at her funeral, Jo Ann's family said they had never seen such a godly, Christian woman. Since her death, Durcie has continued to influence people for good, as other preachers and I have shared her story with thousands of people. Her purpose was to serve God, and God did something great with her life. She was just a sick, little widow, but what a great world this would be if all of us lived with the same love and purpose! Durcie had integrity born of the character she developed by serving God.

What about you? Do you know what purpose God has for your life? It is average people just like you and me, common people, ordinary people, that God can use to restore the upward movement in our country, if we are willing. Are you willing? Paul said, in Philippians 4:13, "I can do everything through him who gives me strength." People like you and me make a force for good that becomes the answer to the problems our country faces. If we will live as people of integrity and honor, the downward trend in our nation will turn into a peaceful, upward movement.

GENERATIONAL MORAL DECLINE

They forfeited their youth, their strength, their home life, and, in many cases, their own lives to keep America free. Earning the title of the "Greatest Generation," they sacrificed themselves for a greater cause. When they returned home victorious, the men and the women of the World War II generation brought a new outlook to life in America. They were determined to make life better for the families they loved. With quiet resolve they built homes, improved education, strengthened industries, encouraged new economic growth, and guided our country into a time of peace and prosperity. These people were defined by a strong sense of personal civic duty, a belief in the permanence of marriage, and an intense loyalty to jobs, schools, and churches.

If this is the "Greatest Generation," does that imply that future generations will decline? Will there never be another great generation? The purpose of this book is to honor the "Greatest Generation" by motivating future generations to build upon the principles of integrity, commitment, and courage so they too will become even greater in their service to our country and our world.

The ingredients that formed the heart of the following generation, known as the baby boomers, changed from sacrifice and commitment to wealth and pleasure. Enjoying the moment became more important to the baby boomers than building for the future. This generation became the "Me Generation." Free love and nonviolent protests ushered in attitudes of self-righteousness and self-centeredness. The self-centeredness quickly fashioned a "buy-now-pay-later generation." During this generation, divorce reached epidemic proportions. From 1960 to 1975, divorces in the US increased from 393,000 to over 1.1 million per year. More time was focused on self, and less time was devoted to children.[1] While the economy blossomed and the glory of the nation increased, there was a change in the hearts of our countrymen. Families began to break apart, and parents reared their children without purpose. While many great people are a part of the baby boomer generation, the fabric of society was shifting from an outward focus to an inward one. There was no longer a greater purpose or a higher call, and the hearts of America's people slowly began to change. Responsibility for the greater good was replaced by the desire to please oneself.

If it is true that the foundation of our lives and our country is the home, this generation, which failed to build solid homes, started the decline of our moral values. We might consider this the real beginning of what Drs. Rick and Kathy Hicks refer to as the tidal wave of negative values.[2] In their book *Boomers, Xers, and Other Strangers*, the Hickses describe the downward movement of values in our society as a great tidal wave leading our country toward greater moral decline. Families with changing values have replaced the traditional families of the 1920s. As

---

[1] George Barna, *The Future of the American Family* (Chicago, Ill.: Moody Press, 1993), 67.
[2] Rick Hicks and Kathy Hicks, *Boomers, Xers, and Other Strangers* (Wheaton, Ill.: Tyndale House Publishers, 1999), 232.

EXAMINING AMERICA'S MORAL DECLINE

the devastating tsunami of December 2004 demonstrated, a tidal wave can be incredibly destructive and impossible to stop. If history repeats itself in our country, the tidal wave of changing values is one that we must stop. History records that nations have a life expectancy of about two hundred years, and we are getting old!

Jim DeMint often displays a graph which he devised around the concepts of Sir Alex Fraser Tyler. (See Chart 1 at the end of the chapter.) A nineteenth-century Scottish historian, Tyler claimed that great civilizations run in two-hundred-year cycles, taking the same path to the top and back, beginning and ending with bondage. If America wakes up, insists DeMint, there is still time to alter the cycle.[3]

The tidal wave of negative values threatens the very fiber of our society. (See Chart 2.)[4] In this book, I will try to cause a small ripple in the water by casting in a stone called integrity. If you have ever thrown a stone into a lake, you have seen how the ripples get larger and larger as they spread out from the point of contact. You and I are the points of contact. The ripples of our lives can grow into increasingly larger circles as we encourage others to stand with us against the tidal wave. When the ripples get large enough, the water will subside into the peaceful harmony of a great and strong nation, standing for moral principles.

As the tidal wave continued to grow and gain strength, as homes broke apart and society became more focused on self and less focused on the good of others, Generation X entered the picture. This generation, following the self-centered example of baby boomers, has produced some distressing trends. William J. Bennett reported in a 1993 *Wall Street Journal* article that "between 1966 and 1993 violent crime increased by 560 percent, illegitimate births increased 419 percent, the number of children living in single-parent homes tripled, and the teenage suicide rate increased more than 300 percent."[5] Simultaneously, SAT

---

[3]Ibid., 230.
[4]Adapted from Hicks and Hicks, 229.
[5]William J. Bennett, "Quantifying America's Decline," *Wall Street Journal*, 15 March 1993.

scores dropped an average of almost 80 points. Our little ripple in the water, integrity, will help us to re-establish homes built on unity, fidelity, and love. As these homes once again become the norm for American life, the ripples of these positive values will grow stronger.

As dissatisfaction with life continued to grow, the next generation was confronted with even greater problems when violence erupted in schools resulting in tragedies such as the Columbine shootings. This new generation has been referred to as the "Net Generation" or the "Disconnected Generation." Primarily reared in single-parent homes, or in homes with both parents gone the majority of time, this generation has trouble building lasting relationships.[6]

Family time for this generation means time watching videos or DVDs. While this generation has exhibited a more positive outlook toward its own abilities, it also has a greater fear of the future, including concerns about terrorism and the possibility of a failing economy. Although members of this generation display a greater concern for family than the past generation, they are short on loyalty and struggle with long-term commitments to jobs, churches, and families. The dominant thought process is: "All values are relative, so one must exhibit tolerance of all people and all lifestyles." As Dr. Hicks points out, "This characteristic may become their greatest downfall." He states, "While a certain level of tolerance is necessary in a diverse society such as ours, the downside of extreme tolerance is that if you don't stand for something, you may fall for anything."[7] As the tidal wave continues to threaten our shores, we calmly add a ring of courage as our little ripple of peace and purpose expands. Courage brings confidence and discipline into our society as people who stand for truth develop the courage to speak out to defend our families and our homes. This courage, however, must never be like the tidal wave, which is rough and uncaring. Truth can only have an impact in restoring the upward

---

[6]Josh McDowell, *The Disconnected Generation* (Nashville, Tenn.: Word Publishing, 2000), 9.
[7]Hicks and Hicks, 230.

movement of our country when it is presented with strength and the gentle touch of both love and compassion. As the apostle Paul explains in Romans 12:21, "Do not be overcome by evil, but overcome evil with good." The N-Geners provide us with hope to stop the tidal wave, but with their attitude of misguided tolerance the question is, "Do they have any beliefs that are strong enough to stand up for at any cost?"

It will be our goal to examine how we can raise the standard for this generation and future generations in order to produce another truly great generation. Can you make a difference? Think about what Durcie accomplished. You have a better education than Durcie. You are younger than Durcie. You are stronger than Durcie. You have more money than Durcie. You know more people than Durcie. If God can influence thousands of lives through Durcie, just think what He can do with your life!

SUMMARY

Over the past fifty years the tidal wave of negative values has eroded the shores of America to the point that our people have lost the real meaning of life. We can no longer look at a great generation that is driven by purpose and principle. We have drifted from a nation with the strong vision of freedom and a great concern for others to a nation of selfishness and separation from others. With each generation our moral values will continue to decline unless we start a movement against the tidal wave. This movement will not seem as powerfully dramatic as the overpowering, nationwide tidal wave of immorality and wickedness, but it will heal our nation with the calm assurance of God's blessings. This movement will begin like the ripples that arise in a lake when a small stone is thrown into it. As the stone hits the water, each succeeding ripple gets larger and larger until it covers the entire lake. (See Chart 3.)

We will be casting the first stone in the lake by developing personal integrity. The people of integrity in this country number in the hundreds of thousands, and those people have the power to impact the communities in which they live. As each person of integrity touches the lives of people around him or her, others will begin to develop an understanding of the importance of good character.

Integrity, however, cannot become the norm in our nation's people until good people become courageous people. For that reason, the second ripple in the water will be increasing the level of moral courage that our people possess. People of strong moral values must not only possess those values, they must be willing to stand in opposition to those who would destroy our morals.

The first place our moral courage can affect is our homes. This becomes the third ring of our widening wave of influence. If the people in my home understand right and wrong, morality and immorality, and also truth and justice, we will not only have a happy family, we will be able to impact the lives of others in our community.

When people of moral courage begin to speak out and to live their values, they will impact the character development in our schools. Character development based on sound moral principles becomes the fourth ring in our widening wave of influence. Parents, teachers, and students all have the right and the responsibility of standing for what they believe during the school year. We must not allow the "intellectual elite" to define our local moral values or to form our worldview. The fifth and most important ring of our ripple of peace is the one that will enable us, gently but firmly, to divert the power of the tidal wave of negative values. We will derive great personal peace when the values of our lives are firmly supported by the absolute truth of God's Word as revealed in the Bible.

Once we have instilled these ideals in our lives, you and I will become a powerful force in the struggle to restore the greatness of America. God will empower us with His awesome strength as we transform the turmoil of declining values into the peace and tranquility of godly values.

STUDY GUIDE: CHAPTER 1
EXAMINING AMERICA'S MORAL DECLINE

I. Discuss the following passages:
   A. Proverbs 22:1: "A good name is more desirable than great riches; to be esteemed is better than silver or gold."
      1. If given the choice between a good reputation and one million dollars, which do you think most people would take? Why?
      2. Now that you have given the "church answer," which would you take?
   B. Psalm 15:1–5
      1. What does it mean to have a blameless walk?
      2. How does a person speak truth from the heart?
      3. Do you think it is strange that a righteous person despises a vile man?
      4. Does this concept agree with Christian love?

II. Discuss the claims about the "Greatest Generation."
   A. Is the World War II generation really the "Greatest Generation"?
   B. Why or why not?
   C. What impact has their generation had on your generation?

III. What do you think about other generations?
   A. What do you think about the illustration of the tidal wave of negative values?
   B. Which of these negative values has had the most devastating effect on people?

IV. How can positive values help stop the tidal wave?
   A. How would you define integrity?
   B. Share thoughts about people you have known who have true integrity.
   C. What is moral courage?
   D. Share illustrations of times when you have seen moral courage demonstrated.

E. In general, how would you describe the health of the average American family?

V. Possible goals of the class
   A. What do you hope to accomplish in this class?
   B. How will your actions help turn back the tidal wave of negative values?

VI. Examining your community
   A. What are the four biggest problems in your community?
   B. What are some ways you can impact your community to overcome these problems?
   C. What are the four biggest problems in your personal life?
   D. Describe the actions you can take to correct those problems.
   E. What is your personal mission in life? (This will be discussed in more detail in a later chapter.)

EXAMINING AMERICA'S MORAL DECLINE

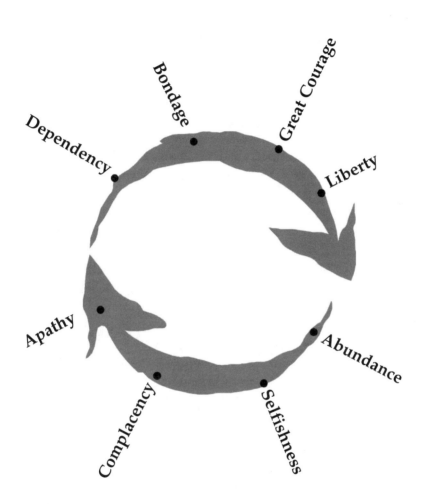

CHART 1

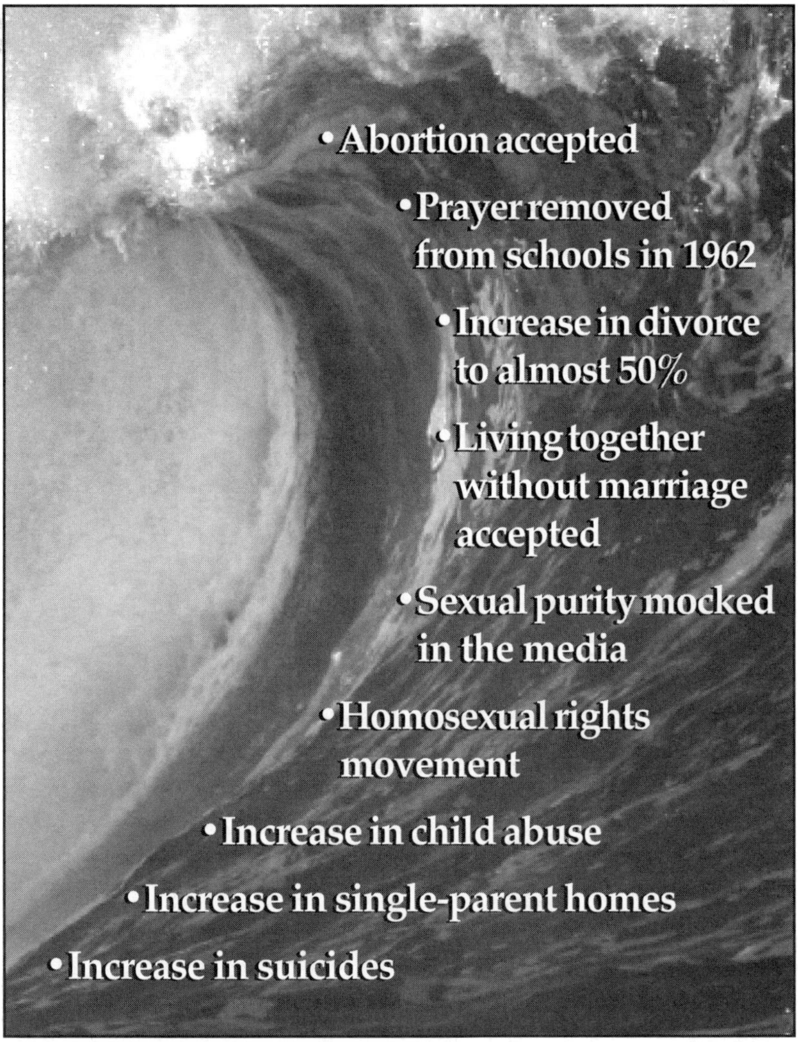

- Abortion accepted
- Prayer removed from schools in 1962
- Increase in divorce to almost 50%
- Living together without marriage accepted
- Sexual purity mocked in the media
- Homosexual rights movement
- Increase in child abuse
- Increase in single-parent homes
- Increase in suicides

CHART 2

EXAMINING AMERICA'S MORAL DECLINE

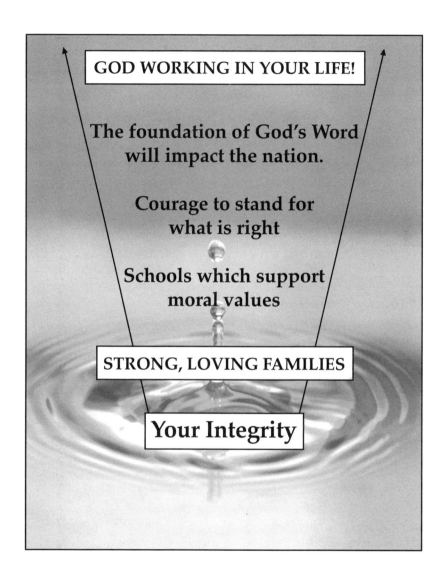

CHART 3

STEP ONE:
ENERGIZING PEOPLE
OF INTEGRITY

2
THE KIDNAPPING OF OUR INTEGRITY!

Integrity! We love the concept but when push comes to shove we would rather be on the winning team!

Ronnie was the best high school football player in Arkansas. He was so good that during a game with a district rival, as he fielded a punt on our five-yard line and retreated into the end zone, I turned to another coach and said, "He's gone." Sure enough, he returned the punt ninety-five yards for a touchdown.

Ronnie's athletic ability was incredible, causing the fans in our little town to want him to play under Lou Holtz at the University of Arkansas. Since Ronnie was the best athlete our community had ever seen, people wanted to make sure he had his chance to play football. In fact, everyone wanted so badly for him to play that the superintendent of schools ordered the school counselor to reorganize the way grades were given in physical education so Ronnie's grade point average would be higher. When Ronnie still couldn't qualify academically for the university, the head coach allowed him to take a special class. Ronnie received an A in the class, although, to my knowledge, the class only met a few times.

The important thing, it seemed, was to make sure that Ronnie could qualify for his scholarship. Anything Ronnie wanted, he was given—including special grades and a little extra spending money from well-meaning townspeople. It was not just our little town that rewarded Ronnie for his athletic ability. As the year progressed, he visited a number of universities, returning with new clothes, spending money, and other incentives.

A year later, the town was overjoyed when Ronnie made the starting team for the Razorbacks. You could feel the excitement in our little town as everyone prepared to see Ronnie play against Oklahoma in the Orange Bowl. It was going to be wonderful: a boy from our little town making national headlines in the Orange Bowl—wonderful, that is, if he hadn't been dismissed from the team for molesting a girl in the dorm.

Our boy never played in the Orange Bowl; in fact, he never played another football game. Ronnie had learned the wrong lesson: Winning is more important than integrity. If you are a great athlete, the rules don't apply to you. It doesn't matter what kind of person you are as long as you can win. Not only was Ronnie dismissed from the team, he was also kicked out of the university. The result, it appears, was a wasted life.

That same year, Tom was a starting guard on our team. He was small, slow, and very average in ability. He was neither an outstanding athlete nor an impressive student. He was, however, a young man with great integrity. Very few people were overly interested in where Tom would go to college or what he would do after high school.

However, that didn't bother Tom. He had other things on his mind. Tom, who rode an early bus to school every day, would walk across the school grounds to the elementary school where he would meet a special child. This little boy lived in a squalid home with only his alcoholic father, who neglected him. He would come to school daily smelling so badly that the teachers couldn't stand to have him in the classroom. Tom would take him to the field house, clean him up, put clean clothing on him, and send him back to his class.

With that kind of character, it was no surprise that Tom worked his way through college, married a fine Christian girl, and became a respected teacher, husband, father, and citizen. In contrast, the last time anyone mentioned Ronnie, they just said that when they saw him, he was drunk. Which one was the real winner? Would you consider the great athlete or the young man with great integrity to be the more successful? Which one do you want as your neighbor?

If our country is going to restore the upward movement of future generations, we must value integrity above winning, wealth, or worldly success. Integrity—we love the idea, but have trouble with the practice. Dr. Steven Carter, in his 1996 book entitled *Integrity*, states, "In a nutshell, America's integrity dilemma is that we are full of fine talk about how desperately our society needs it, but when push comes to shove, we would just as soon be on the winning side."[1]

We can identify five major reasons why we have become a nation that loves to talk about integrity while continuing to live with less and less of it in our lives. Very slowly, very discreetly, working below the surface of our understanding, five devious changes in our thinking have kidnapped the integrity of our people. The first are the insidious mixed messages received by every person in our society as we are told to be honest, to play by the rules, and yet people who break the rules are rewarded for their accomplishments. Second, the concept that our moral views must be kept out of public life has quietly but effectively removed the voice of thousands of good people from the political arena. As people of integrity have been silenced in the political arena, we face a third powerful enemy, a misunderstood perception of tolerance. Many people with great moral values now believe they must tolerate any lifestyle, regardless of the damage it may to do our society. As with any kidnapping, fear is a part of the equation. In a society that values tolerance above morality, if a person speaks up for his or her values, the result will certainly be negative. Since none of us like to suffer ridicule, we have chosen to become the silent majority in regard to our ethical views. The fifth element makes the kidnapping complete. We can no longer have any form of integrity when we are completely unable to understand truth as opposed to falsehood. Our postmodern relativity is capable of removing the last strand of our integrity.

DOUBLE MESSAGES

Our desire to develop personal integrity is overpowered by the double messages which we receive every day in our society. We encourage our children to show good sportsmanship, but consider the following scenario: During a football game, the ball

---

[1]Steven Carter, *Integrity* (New York: Harper/Collins Publishers, 1996), 4.

is thrown to a receiver, and it clearly hits the ground before it gets to the receiver, who scoops it off the turf. When the referee calls it a legal catch, the announcers rave about the heads-up play of the receiver who acted as if he caught the ball.

Where is our integrity? We should be saying, "Look at that young man! He's a liar, a cheat, and a disgrace to his school." However, since winning has become more important than integrity, our children receive mixed messages: We want you to play fair, but if you have a chance, cheat to win. This backdoor message will overflow into every aspect of their lives, and our children will lack integrity and honesty.

Backdoor messages destroy integrity!

You remember Mary Kay LeTourneau, the teacher who had sexual relations with a twelve-year-old boy in her class. Barbara Walters did an interview with her on *20/20*, questioning her about the relationship. The interview, however, did not center around the devastating effects her actions had on her own four children, or the way her husband suffered because of her actions, or even the confusion it would cause her other students. The interview was centered on LeTourneau and the fact that she "really loved this boy." The interview was presented in such a way that, although LeTourneau had to spend seven and a half years in jail and had adversely affected the lives of everyone around her, if you talked with her, you would really see that she was a good person who was just misunderstood. By the end of the program, the audience was feeling sorry for the woman who had taken advantage of a twelve-year-old and destroyed her own family.

Double messages confuse our thinking and adversely affect our morality. The focus should have been on LeTourneau's responsibility to her four [now six] children and her responsibility to her husband. We should also examine how her bad example affected the lives of her students.

MISGUIDED CONCEPT: KEEP MORALITY OUT OF PUBLIC LIFE

Our second struggle with integrity comes from the misguided concept that we should keep morality out of public life. Steven Carter argues, "Today's political talk about how it is wrong for government to enforce one person's morality on somebody else is just mindless chatter. Every law enforces one person's morality on somebody else. Because law has only two functions; to tell people to do what they would rather not or to forbid them from doing what they would."[2]

Some people are fond of saying, "You are what you eat." In truth, both as individuals and as a nation, we are what we believe. "As water reflects a face, so a man's heart reflects the man" (Prov. 27:19). You cannot respond to any situation without reflecting on the principles that you have accepted all of your life. Without realizing it, those who claim we should keep morality out of public life are actually instigating the foundation for an amoral society.

An amoral society is one in which there is *no* standard by which people are expected to live. In that form of society, every action depends solely on the whim of the individual. Everything is viewed as acceptable if the individuals involved feel good about it. Problems develop when those desires, which feel good to one person, become harmful to another person. As the conflict between individuals grows, either a standard is imposed, or there is anarchy and the strongest person wins.

In an amoral society, there is no absolute truth; truth changes according to the will of the individual. The conclusion of keeping morals out of public life is that whoever is the strongest will eventually be considered right. If that philosophy is correct, consider this prospect. Adolf Hitler was stronger than the Jews in Germany, so he must have been right in exterminating them. Although our moral values would tell us that murdering people is wrong, we *must*, so we are told, keep our moral values out of

---

[2]Ibid.

public life. I don't really believe many *thinking* Americans would buy into that philosophy. To be people of integrity, we must have values (moral standards) that benefit people in our society. Our votes and our comments will be directed by those moral standards as we use them to elect government officials. They will also become the basis for our personal involvement in the political arena.

MISUNDERSTANDING—
THE CONCEPT OF TOLERANCE

In our society, the concept of *tolerance* is greatly misunderstood and is rapidly destroying our integrity. If we are to be people of integrity, all of us have a responsibility to be kind and courteous to other people. That does *not* mean we must accept lifestyles that are damaging to us or to our nation. At work, at school, and in the marketplace, we have the right to speak up for what we believe. If we are silent, more and more destructive concepts gain acceptance in our society.

Tolerance has become the death knell of the truth!

While homosexuals make up only 2 percent of our population, homosexuals commit over 30 percent of all child abuse![3] In our attempts to be tolerant and not offend anyone, these facts have not been discussed, so we are shocked and surprised when we learn the truth. Personally, I believe it is offensive to see children being abused while we refuse to admit that this segment of society has increased the problem. When Christian people are required to work side by side with people living an immoral lifestyle, with the fear of being punished if they speak against a damaging lifestyle, tolerance becomes an excuse to force the

---

[3]Kurt Freund, G. Heasman, L. G. Racansky, G. Clancy, "Pedophilia and Heterosexuality vs. Homosexuality," *Journal of Sex and Marital Therapy* 10 (Fall 1984): 198. The proportional prevalence of offenders against male children in this group of 457 offenders against children was 36 percent. The same article notes that the vast majority of sexual abuse is done by males.

acceptance of ideals that are harmful to our society.

FEAR OF CONSEQUENCES

A fourth challenge to our integrity stems from our fear of the consequences of standing up for what we believe. In 1993, *60 Minutes* producer Lowell Bergman received information concerning the damaging effects of tobacco that had been carefully hidden by the tobacco companies. His information came from Dr. Jeffrey Wigland, a disgruntled former executive who had been fired by a tobacco company. When Dr. Wigland blew the whistle on Brown and William Tobacco Company, there was retribution. He lost his job, faced lawsuits, endured death threats, and the pressure even caused him to lose his family. However, a 236-million-dollar lawsuit was won against the company for its attempts to hide the effects of nicotine on people. Dr. Wigland became an award-winning teacher, founded the nonprofit organization "Smoke-Free Kids," and inspired the movie *The Insider*.[4] However, his long, hard battle with the company included some difficult times. It is the loss of a job, income, and social standing that we fear.

Larry Johnson, in his book *Absolute Honesty: Building a Corporate Climate that Values Straight Talk and Rewards Integrity*, lists the following consequences that a person might face when he stands up for what he believes:

1. Retribution
2. Fear of hurting someone's feelings
3. Fear of change
4. Being disliked
5. Loss of support
6. Paying the price
7. Losing the competitive edge
8. Losing face[5]

---

[4]Larry Johnson and Bob Phillips, *Absolute Honesty: Building a Corporate Culture that Values Straight Talk and Rewards Integrity* (New York: AMACOM Books, 2003), 56.

[5]Ibid., 67.

My daughter Kelly is a licensed professional counselor working for a telephone counseling service designed to help employees of large companies when they experience emotional problems. As a counselor, she is required to attend continuing education classes. During one such class, the instructor, who was dressed as a man, announced that she was a cross-dressing lesbian. When the class began it was quickly apparent that the instructor had a large axe to grind against "narrow-minded churches and narrow-minded Christians." Although Kelly and several other people in the class disagreed with what she had to say, they were required to be politically correct and listen for three hours as Christians and our beliefs were continually bashed. If any of them had spoken up, they would have been risking their jobs and possibly their licenses.

Shortly after the class, I received a call from Kelly. We discussed the ways Christians could respond in this type of situation, and how she could make her grievance known to her employer. Her employer, by the way, is a Christian man who may not have even been aware of the things being taught in the class. If it is wrong for Christians to discriminate against immoral people, is it not also wrong for immoral people to discriminate against Christians?

If it is wrong for Christians to discriminate against immoral people, is it not also wrong for immoral people to discriminate against Christians?

Our society has turned so far away from God that we are now afraid to stand up for what we believe. Reverse discrimination seems to have become acceptable as those who push for their rights are continuously attacking the rights of those who believe in God and His moral law. It is time we firmly, but lovingly, stand up for our rights as Christians who are also citizens of the United States of America.

THE KIDNAPPING OF OUR INTEGRITY!

LACK OF UNDERSTANDING OF THE NATURE OF TRUTH

A fifth reason we struggle to maintain integrity is that we do not understand the nature of truth. In response to a Barna Research Group survey question: "Is there absolute truth?" 65 percent said there is no such thing as absolute truth; different people can define "truth" in conflicting ways and still be correct.[6] Seventy-two percent of Baby Busters believe that there is no absolute truth.[7]

Where there is no absolute,
there is no foundation for life!

If we are to get this country back on solid ground, we must understand that, when there is no absolute, there is no place to stand. It is similar to living our lives on sinking sand. When there is a problem, no one can solve it. After all, my solution is as good as yours, since there is no standard. Think about our financial system. What kind of chaos would exist in America if all states didn't use the same monetary system? Think about it: I could say my one-dollar bill is worth as much as your one-thousand-dollar bill. No one can say I'm wrong. No monetary system can work without an absolute standard. If we are to restore integrity to our country, we must start with an understanding of truth!

SUMMARY

These five dangerous enemies of integrity have confused us and made it difficult for us to have real integrity. All five of these elements cause doubt, and doubt is the enemy of integrity. It takes great confidence to stand up for what you believe; when-

---

[6]George Barna, *What Americans Believe* (Chicago, Ill.: Moody Press, 1993), 83.
[7]Ibid.

ever you begin to doubt, you will begin to slide away from your principles. People can exhibit great moral character only when they are confident of the foundation for their beliefs. People of integrity know right from wrong, and they are able to respond to situations in their life accordingly. Double messages, misguided concepts of tolerance, faith's absence from public life, the fear of consequences, and a lack of understanding of truth—all undermine the confidence of good people.

STUDY GUIDE: CHAPTER 2
THE KIDNAPPING OF OUR INTEGRITY!

I. Discuss the following passages:
   A. Proverbs 10:9: "The man of integrity walks securely, but he who takes crooked paths will be found out."
      1. When you were young, did you ever do anything you didn't want to tell your parents?
      2. What kind of pressure did you feel? Did it make you nervous or anxious?
      3. Why do you think the person of integrity has peace of mind and security?
   B. Proverbs 11:3: "The integrity of the upright guides them, but the unfaithful are destroyed by their duplicity."
      1. What does duplicity mean?
      2. Why would it destroy a person?
      3. How does integrity guide a person in his or her decisions?
   C. Proverbs 29:10: "Bloodthirsty men hate a man of integrity and seek to kill the upright."
      1. Why do evil people hate men and women of integrity?
      2. How do people in the world show their hatred of Christians?
      3. What evidence do you see of discrimination against Christians in America today?

II. Considering integrity
   A. Do you agree with the Steven Carter's comment that Americans love the concept of integrity, "but when push

comes to shove, we would just as soon be on the winning side"?
   B. How would *you* define "integrity"?

III. Why do people lack integrity?
   A. What double messages are Americans receiving that would harm our personal integrity?
   B. How do those messages affect our children and us?
   C. Do you agree with this statement? "Our morals must be a part of our public lives because we are what we believe." Why do you agree or disagree?
   D. What do you think about the statement that "tolerance has become the death knell of the truth"?
   E. What would you consider a proper approach to the concept of tolerance?
   F. In what ways have you seen fear keep people from standing for what they believe?
   G. What is your view of truth? Is there such a thing as absolute truth?

IV. Developing personal integrity.
   A. Keep a record of the double messages you receive during the next few weeks.
   B. List your own fears that keep you from standing up for your faith.
   C. Give an account of a time when you made a solid stand for something you believed in. How did it make you feel?
   D. Set up a time for your family to discuss the factors that can damage their integrity.
   E. Spend time praying with your family for integrity.

3
ENERGIZING PEOPLE OF INTEGRITY

**People who lack integrity are changed
by the circumstances of their lives, while people
of integrity change their circumstances
by acting on their principles.**

Gary was shocked when his twenty-year-old daughter came into his house and announced she was moving in with her boyfriend. Now, most Christian people I know would have been upset, but they wouldn't have made a stand. Gary, however, was a man of integrity who could not teach against immorality and still allow it in his own family. He had a long talk with his daughter explaining to her how much her parents loved her. Always remember, we overcome evil with good, which means we approach difficult situations with firmness controlled by love.

Gary also explained the eternal consequences of his daughter's lifestyle choice and asked her to repent. She refused to listen to his encouragement. When she refused, he took one the most courageous stands I have ever seen a father take. He firmly explained to her that although he and his wife loved her with all their hearts, she was no longer welcome in their home. Until she repented, neither she nor her boyfriend would be welcomed home for Thanksgiving, Christmas, or any other family gathering.

When she left angry and defiant, it broke his heart. He and his wife cried and prayed for their daughter for the next two years. Then one remarkable evening there was a knock at the door. With tears in her eyes, their daughter begged for their forgiveness as she explained that she was leaving the boyfriend and repenting of her immoral lifestyle. She is now a faithful Christian who has a home of her own, dedicated to God. Integrity requires the courage to make a stand for our principles, even when it hurts! I'm not sure I would have had that much courage, but I know that Gary is a man of great integrity.

What do you think about Gary's action? Was he too harsh? Shouldn't he have shown more grace? Wasn't he taking a chance of losing his daughter? You and I have a lot of questions we might ask about his actions. However, everything that Christ teaches about real love was present in his actions. He had always loved his daughter and would always love her. She came to realize that he would never intentionally hurt her; in fact, she grew to understand that he was trying to help her. She also knew that when she repented, he would rejoice and forgive her. Sounds a lot like the way Jesus responds to us, doesn't it? We need to understand the strength of life-changing love!

If we are to save our nation from these despicable kidnappers and the tidal wave of negative values they have produced, we must start a ripple of integrity. Starting a gentle wave of positive values will require a solid understanding of the concept of integrity. When we fully understand the thoughts and actions required to become people of integrity, we will be capable of implementing an uncomplicated four-step plan to restore our integrity.

A great first step will be rediscovering the old-fashioned principles of respect, courtesy, and a positive approach to life and relationships. This approach to everyday life will become a solid foundation for the development of integrity and good character. Children who learn respect and courtesy generally become adults who are outstanding citizens.

The second step in the development of integrity comes from our inner motivation. What worthwhile purpose is God going to accomplish in our lives? Motivation is always a key to success in life's important adventures. However, just knowing the right values is not enough; we must be willing to take action on those principles.

Action becomes the third step in our plan to ignite the integrity of our people. We cannot wait for someone else to do something. We all need to take to heart the old saying, "If it is to be, it's up to me."

The final step is to gain involvement from other good, morally-strong people in our communities. I firmly believe that there are more good people in our country than evil ones. When motivated by truth, your community can determine its own destiny in regard to moral values.

You can help develop young people who will be great leaders. You can elect city and county officials who have high standards. You can build a remarkable, morally-strong community if you are willing to get your friends and neighbors involved. *Remember, they share your concerns!*

UNDERSTANDING INTEGRITY

In order to rebuild integrity in our country, a good understanding of the concept of personal integrity is essential. Dr. Steven Carter explains integrity as a three-step process:

1. Discerning what is right and what is wrong.
2. Acting on what you have discerned, even at personal cost.
3. Saying openly that you are acting on your understanding of right from wrong.[1]

Elaborating on these aspects of integrity, we quickly notice that integrity involves understanding, acting, and speaking. Since our society proclaims, "Your truth is as good as my truth," acquiring the knowledge upon which our integrity will be developed becomes extremely difficult. Is there any real truth? If there is, where can I find it? Our answer will be formulated from what we believe to be the only real guiding truth of the universe: God.

The vast majority of Americans believe that there is a God who created the universe. In fact, according to a 2003 Harris poll, 90 percent of Americans believe in a higher power.[2] It seems

---

[1] Steven Carter, *Integrity* (New York: Harper/Collins, 1996), 7.
[2] George Barna, *The Future of the American Family* (Chicago, Ill.: Moody Press, 1993), 30.

logical that this higher power has set into motion principles designed to allow his creation to function in a civilized manner. The teachings of the Bible, beginning with the Ten Commandments and continuing through the marvelous, loving teachings of Jesus Christ, provide a solid foundation upon which society can be built.

The second part of Dr. Carter's definition illustrates that integrity cannot exist if a person does not *act* upon the solid foundation he or she has learned. Shortly after my son Keith got his driver's license, we had an ice storm. Keith was totally unprepared to drive without the benefit of good traction. While he was at work one afternoon, the ice storm hit, and he immediately called for advice. I responded by saying, "Keith, drive slowly. I mean very slowly. Whatever you think is slow, go slower. Keith, did you get my point? I mean really, really slowly." Within twenty minutes he called back, "Dad, I should have driven slower. I just slid over a stop sign. What do I do now?"

If you have ever driven a car on ice, you know how important it is to have a good base for traction. If tires on the car are spinning without making contact with anything substantial, you will quickly lose control. If the only foundation we have is ourselves, we will be like tires slipping on ice: Our society will quickly spin out of control. Without a solid base, there is no way to know where it will go or when it will stop. We cannot be people of integrity and act on what we believe if our belief system constantly changes according to our current circumstances.

> *People who lack integrity are always changed by the circumstances of their lives, while people of integrity change their circumstances by acting on their principles.*

It is not good enough just to know the truth; we must live according to those truth principles. Every day, good, moral people are compromising their faith in God in order to be accepted in our rapidly changing society. When everyone around you cheats on his taxes, you, a person of integrity, will not. When other businesses find small ways to make money with catch-phrases or false advertising, your business maintains total honesty. When others simply overlook immorality in our society, you, the person of integrity, stand up against it. To stop the directionless spinning of society, the rubber must meet the road, and we must stand for what we really believe.

Many of us, as Americans, are failing in regard to the third part of Carter's definition of integrity. We are afraid to speak up for what we believe. Although we have a foundation of truth in our personal lives, we have not translated those principles into our public lives. We have not been brave enough to speak up and let people know where we stand on important issues. We are allowing our country to decay because we refuse to speak up against those ideas and behaviors destroying our homes and our families.

Recently I became involved in some activities designed to protect our homes from the increasing danger of the false information being presented by homosexual activists. As we will observe later, in the chapter on the home, the distorted information provided to our young people in schools about the homosexual lifestyle, coupled with a misapplied concept of tolerance, is helping to destroy morality in our country. Sadly, when I presented the concepts to a group of church leaders, several of them pulled me aside and said: "We have already lost that battle. It is better just to be quiet." Whenever we refuse to do what is right because we have given up, that, my friends, is a lack of integrity! People of integrity will speak up for truth regardless of the consequences or the possibility of losing the struggle. The reality is that even if we lose the immediate battle, God ultimately *will* win. We will have done the right thing, and our personal integrity will be reinforced.

RESTORING INTEGRITY

1. Restore Respect, Courtesy, and a Positive Attitude

The first step in restoring integrity in our country is to restore respect and courtesy, coupled with a positive attitude about life. Hold on—for the past thirty pages, I have been describing huge problems in our country. After discussing problems with the power to shake the fabric of our lives, why would we start with such a simple solution? It really doesn't appear to make sense. The following is one of the most powerful concepts you will ever learn. This one principle, which helps explain how God works in our lives, will change your perspective on all of life's problems. Simply stated, *while life's problems are extremely complex, the solutions are quite simple!*

When I first met John, his speech impressed me. He said "Yes, sir," or "Yes, ma'am," whenever he addressed another adult. When I observed him more closely, it became obvious that he treated his wife and his daughter with great courtesy as well. His respect for other people became even more apparent whenever John was involved in a work project at church. He was always there on time, prepared to work, with a smile on his face.

While life's problems are extremely complex, the solutions are quite simple!

It was John's early training that made him such a man of integrity. Early training from parents who know what they believe in and are willing to guide their children in the development of a clear conscience will set a pattern for their lives.

In his book *The Moral Intelligence of Children*, Robert Coles interviewed young girls who began their involvement in sexual activity by the age of ten and planned to be mothers by fourteen. He also interviewed young people in their early teens who had already decided that doing drugs was the only way out of their unhappy lives. In his research, he learned one simple fact: *Children are looking for moral guidance.* They *want* to know how to behave in the adult world. They are looking directly at their parents for a pattern and direction. Mr. Coles asserts that moral intelligence isn't acquired only by memorization of rules and regulations. We grow morally as a direct consequence of witnessing grown-up morality, *or the lack of it.*[3] Children are always

---

[3]Robert Coles, *The Moral Intelligence of Children* (New York: Random House, 1997), 5.

looking for clues from adults concerning how to behave in the world.

Morris Massey, in his book *The People Puzzle*, defines three important stages of value development.[4] In the first stage, at ages one through seven, a child begins to develop values from observation or patterning. Since children primarily observe parents and family members, their first introduction to the principles by which they will live comes from the family. The second stage, from approximately ages eight through thirteen, is the age of modeling heroes. This stage can be extremely important in the final formation of an individual's life, as Massey discovered while teaching a graduate class. During the class he found that 13 out of 15 students were pursuing careers similar to those of their childhood heroes.

Who are your children's heroes? Do you know? Now is a good time to stop and evaluate who the heroes are for our children in today's society. A few years back, before television, computers, and video games, a child's hero was almost always a family member or a community leader. But who is it today? What do you think of the moral values of those heroes?

During the third stage, peers become the molding instruments for our values. This stage, referred to as the socialization period, usually takes place from ages fourteen to twenty, as young people grow away from the influence of parents and begin to experience shared values with their closest friends. Massey suggests that at the end of this third period, the values one lives by are set for the rest of one's life. Unless there is some form of "significant emotional event" which occurs later in life, they will probably never be swayed from these values. *Integrity must be developed at a young age!*

The training of our children begins with showing respect for people in the way we talk. As the writer of Proverbs said, "The tongue has the power of life and death . . ." (Prov. 18:21a). Jesus also told us, "For out of the overflow of the heart the mouth speaks" (Mt. 12:34b). James explained to us that if we can con-

---

[4]Morris Massey, *The People Puzzle: Understanding Yourself and Others* (Reston, Va.: Reston Publishing Co., 1979).

trol the tongue we can control the entire body (see Jas. 3:2–12). To restore integrity we begin by changing the way people speak to each other.

On a national news program a few years ago, there was a study which concluded that young people today speak to each other in vulgar and disrespectful ways because that is just a part of their culture. In essence, the conclusion was that adults should just chill out and let the kids be kids. The problem is that every time we speak to others in a vulgar or disrespectful way, we lower their self-image, as we also lower our own self-image. It is pleasant when a conversation is conducted with politeness and honor. If we teach our young people to speak with politeness, they will still be kids; but they will have their minds and hearts set on a higher level.

The second part of the training is common courtesy—the kind of courtesy displayed in opening the door for a lady, and hearing the lady say, "Thank you," in return; saying, "Please," and, "Thank you," when someone does something kind or courteous.

Henry is a retired airline pilot and a man of great integrity. I have observed his life, and his treatment of other people is unique. He addresses people with respect, and he always looks for a way to show kindness and courtesy. Could it be that there is a connection between that respect for other people and the fact that he is a man of integrity? "Above all else, guard your heart, for it is the wellspring of life" (Prov. 4:23).

Unfortunately, a recent online survey indicates that we are not doing very well in this area. Not only do 8 out of 10 Americans in the study say that a lack of respect and courtesy is a serious problem, but 6 out of 10 say things have become worse in recent years. Whether we are shopping, working or involved in leisure activities, a little common courtesy changes the attitude of our society.

Helping our children to develop a positive attitude toward life is our third avenue for developing respect in our society. We live in a negative society. If you don't believe it, just watch television for a few minutes. The news is filled with the world's problems, and the most popular shows are crime-scene dramas filled with blood and wickedness. Even the comedies get their laughs by putting someone down or making someone look foolish. Look at the video games the kids are playing; many of them are violent and mean-spirited. Why not give our children a good perspective on how great life can be? If we have a positive view of life, each day can be a joy rather than a struggle. After all, the Scriptures remind us, "This is the day the Lord has made; let us rejoice and be glad in it" (Ps. 118.24).

Attitude changes reality!

Attitude changes reality! We create our own environment by the way we approach each day of our lives. In a study published in the July 2003 issue of *Psychosomatic Medicine*, researchers compared how often people with either positive or negative emotions contract a cold. Their results indicated that those who are energetic, happy, and relaxed are less likely to catch colds, while those who are depressed, nervous, or angry are more likely to complain about symptoms regardless of whether or not they actually have a cold. In fact, people with these negative attributes were generally more likely to report symptoms of illness than those who have a positive attitude about life. In other words, positive-thinking people create an environment of health in which to live. Attitude creates reality!

If we are to create an environment for growth in the next generation, we must teach our children to ignore the negative people of the world and create their own positive realities. I believe strongly that attitude changes reality because I have seen it in my own life. When I was in high school, I had two goals in life. The first was to play college football. Everyone, including my high school coach, tried to explain to me that I was just too small and too slow to play college football, and they were absolutely right. However, I have some really great memories of the four years I spent playing football at Harding University.

My second goal was to become a preacher. Again, a number of wise people who understood the ministry realized that I was not cut out for the task. Several experienced preachers, along with some other leaders in the church, put their arms around my shoulder and pulled me aside to explain gently that I was too shy and didn't have the speaking ability or people skills needed to be a full-time preacher. The last thirty years of doing exactly what negative thinkers explained I couldn't do have been a great blessing in my life. By the way, some of my best friends and closest advisers have told me that it was a waste of my time to try and write a book. I hope you enjoy this book anyway! If the next generation is to be successful, we must not only teach them to speak kindly, and to act courteously, we must also give them a positive view of life. *Only positive people accomplish their goals!*

By now you should be seeing that the development of these qualities will start our children on a path that leads to a life of integrity. The more they speak with kindness, the more courteous their actions will become; and the more courteous they are to others, the more good they will see in the world around them. As they develop these traits, they will become more and more positive about the blessings of life.

2. Understand Inner Motivation

The second step in developing individual integrity is in understanding the moral principles that guide our lives. Motivation is the key to life. We respond to life according to the source of our inner motivation.

*If the inner motivation is weak,
our lives will be unproductive!*

Real, powerful motivation comes from a purpose greater than ourselves. The question becomes, "What is that purpose?" People struggle with integrity because they do not know what is expected of them. What does it mean to be a person of integrity? Nathan Branden has correctly stated: "Integrity is the integration of ideals, convictions, standards, beliefs and behavior. When our behavior is congruent with our professed values, when ideals and practice match, we have integrity."[5] When we are able to iden-

---

[5]Nathan Branden, *The Six Pillars of Self-Esteem* (New York: Bantam Books, 1995), 143.

tify a standard worthy to live by and live according to that standard, we restore integrity to our society. It is difficult to live up to any standard if we don't understand the standard.

Once, when my daughter was little, she came into the house and expressed herself using vulgar and totally unacceptable words. I immediately responded by taking her to her room and spanking her. I felt great remorse for my actions when she asked, with big tears in her eyes, "But, Daddy, what does that mean?" Kelly was not responsible for her actions because she didn't understand why the words were wrong. I apologized to her and gently explained the reason we didn't use those words. Because most young people today believe that truth is relative and there is no absolute truth, finding a beginning point for integrity can be challenging.

Chapter 11 of this book will deal extensively with the fact that God's Word, the Bible, is the best foundation for our standards. For now, it is important for us to recognize that when practice lives up to expectations, we are people of integrity. When we meet the expectations of our beliefs, we develop great self-esteem and purpose.

In S. Coopersmith's study of adolescent boys raised in alcoholic homes, he states:

> Children develop self-trust, venturesomeness and the ability to deal with adversity if they are treated with respect and are provided with well-defined standards of values, demands for competence, and guidance toward solutions of problems. Children will develop self-reliance if fostered by a well-structured, demanding environment, rather than by largely unlimited permissiveness and freedom to explore in an unfocused way.[6]

As parents, we must take on the responsibility of training our children in an environment of discipline and control, gently

---

[6]S. Coopersmith, "Self-Concept Research Implications for Education," Paper presented to the American Education Research Association, Los Angeles, California, 6 February 1929, xvi.

but firmly leading them to understand truth and how to live according to that truth.

Let your children (and yourself) know that God has created all of us on purpose for a purpose. In Ephesians 1:4, 5, Paul states, "For he chose us in him before the creation of the world to be holy and blameless in his sight. In love he predestined us to be adopted as his sons through Jesus Christ, in accordance with his pleasure and will." What a great thought, that before the creation of the world, God knew your name! He knows what plan He has for your life. Now all you have to do is live up to His plan! Your children are not here by accident; they are here to glorify God. Teach them how important their actions, goals, and accomplishments are to God!

Before we can develop a people of integrity, we must clearly define the principles upon which integrity rests. Nine valuable pillars of integrity are well-defined in Scripture. In the Book of Galatians, the fruit of the Spirit, as defined by Paul, presents a great foundation for integrity. "But the fruit of the Spirit is love, joy, peace, patience, kindness, goodness, faithfulness, gentleness and self-control" (Gal. 5:22, 23a).

When we couple with these principles the Christian graces listed by Peter in II Peter 1:5–8, we have a perfect foundation for a life of dignity.

> For this very reason, make every effort to add to your faith goodness; and to goodness, knowledge; and to knowledge, self-control; and to self-control, perseverance; and to perseverance, godliness; and to godliness, brotherly kindness; and to brotherly kindness, love. For if you possess these qualities in increasing measure, they will keep you from being ineffective and unproductive in your knowledge of our Lord Jesus Christ.

With a foundation of these principles we can begin to mold our character to match our standards.

3. Standing for Those Principles

We must become people who will model integrity for our children by courageously standing for our principles. Philosopher Lynne McFall has argued that there is no integrity without risk of loss:

> A person of integrity is willing to bear the consequences of her convictions, even when this is difficult; that is, when the consequences are unpleasant. If we are never tested, we never really know how deeply we believe; if there is no possibility of its loss, integrity cannot exist. We can never really know whether we are acting from deep and steadfast principles until those principles are tested.[7]

The real challenge is not just to understand integrity; it is to develop the courage to live according to the principles that represent our moral standards. Julie was a girl in my class in elementary school. She was poor, awkward, not very attractive, and a very slow learner. It was a common practice of my friends to laugh at her and tease her during recess. Their torments often resulted in her running back into the school building with huge tears running down her cheeks. Although I never entered into the teasing and often felt sorry for her, I never had the courage to defend her, or to discourage the other boys from hurting her. Knowing what is right but not having the courage to act on it is a lack of integrity.

The immoral minority will control the minds of our children if people of integrity do not have the courage to speak!

As the immoral minority in our society continues to push for ungodly lifestyles and laws in our country, our children will be convinced that they are right if parents lack the integrity to speak

---

[7]Carter, 23.

up. To be people of integrity, we must stand up for what we believe every time we face the challenge of dishonesty, immorality, or other forms of wickedness. This country will never have another great generation unless we become a courageous people.

In order to implement this type of courageous integrity, our children must see as role models adults who cherish integrity more than money, fame, or success. Real success is not found in outside accomplishments; it is found when we control inner thoughts to the degree that we are able to act on our beliefs at any time, regardless of the risk.

I learned a great lesson about integrity when I was a freshman in college. As I have already stated, I was too small and too slow to play college football; however, as a freshman at Harding University, I was able to make the team and earn a scholarship.

Coach John Prock, a man of immense integrity, had the simple rule that if you were a starter, you were given a scholarship. When spring training arrived, the coaches made a change in our defensive alignment and this short, slow boy was suddenly covering fast, tall, talented receivers as a cornerback. I was fighting hard to keep my position when on the sixth day of spring training, a low block from the back took out my right knee.

As I lay in the hospital with a cast up to my hip, the doctor assured me that I would be able to play again. However, he added that the injured knee would probably affect my already slow speed. "Great!" I thought. "Now, I'm small and *extremely* slow!" I had seen a number of the recruits who wanted to play for Harding, and there were some really good athletes with size, speed, and ability.

In an NAIA school during the late 1960s, each school only had thirty-three scholarships available, so it was difficult to recruit top athletes. There was nothing in writing about my scholarship. Coach Prock had simply told me that I would be on a scholarship my sophomore year. When he came to visit me in the hospital, I knew that most coaches would have taken the opportunity to recruit a better athlete and not depend on the possible return of an average player who was hurt. It took all the courage I could muster to ask him about the scholarship.

Coach Prock seemed stunned by the question: "Kilmer, you were a starter when you went down, and starters are on scholarship!"

It was a simple response that taught me a great lesson. Yes, I learned a lot about integrity that day. This was a man under great pressure to win, yet he honored his word, even when the outcome was in question. Since those college years, I have heard many similar stories from other players whose lives were affected by this man who was doing more than winning ball games; he was building men. That is integrity in action!

Consider the impact we will have on the next generation if we can model that same type of integrity for them. Winning is not on the scoreboard; winning is a life of honesty and integrity. Children never forget the important role models in their lives. You can change the next generation by becoming a model of good character.

4. Building Community Support

We must build communities that support the development of good moral character. Once we teach respect and manners to our children, make sure that they understand the difference between right and wrong, and model moral courage for them, it is imperative for us to increase the reinforcement they get in order to develop good character. Reinforcement must come from entire communities that are committed to the moral training of the next generation. This means getting civic clubs, churches, and schools actively involved in character development.

President Ronald Reagan had this to say about education's basic purpose:

> We're beginning to realize, once again, that education at its core is more than just teaching our young the skills that are needed for a job, however important that is. It's also about passing on to each new generation the values that serve as the foundation and cornerstone of our free democratic society—patriotism, loyalty, faithfulness, courage, the ability to make the crucial moral distinctions between right and wrong, the maturity to understand that all that we have and achieve in this world comes

first from a beneficent and loving God.⁸

"Social capital" is the term used for the interaction between people in a community. When neighbors are close and there is a high degree of involvement in school, there is a great deal of social capital. High levels of social capital exist in communities where parents know each other, go to meetings, vote, and know the other kids. However, social capital is declining and becoming almost nonexistent in our country. Growing numbers of dual-working homes and single-parent homes, along with an increase in video games, computer usage, and television watching are increasing the disconnected feelings of youth.⁹

Building communities where people know and support each other is an important key to help us rebuild the moral standards of our nation. If we are to encourage our children to be people of integrity, we must enlist the help of others in our community. When I look around my neighborhood, I see people who share my moral values and standards. When I talk with people in our schools, most of them have the same values, even though some of them complain that they are forced to go against their standards in order to be tolerant of lifestyles that they know are wrong and harmful.

If this country is a democracy, and the majority of people where you live have good moral standards, those values can and should be taught in our schools. The question is, "How do we accomplish that goal?" Let's just cast a pebble into the lake and see what happens.

Since the really big winners in life are not the great athletes but the people who care for others and exhibit good character in their lives, why not get together with a few of your neighbors and organize a scholarship program for "good kids"? There are civic clubs already offering leadership scholarships and character scholarships, but they are only small awards.

---

⁸Steven D. Schafersman, "Teaching Morals and Values in Public Schools, A Humanist Perspective" (March, 1991) [article on-line]; available from http://www.freeinquiry.com.
⁹Katherine S. Newman, *Rampage: The Social Roots of School Shootings* (New York: Basic Books, 2004), 111.

We're not talking about a small award; we're talking about a full ride, a four-year scholarship that is as valuable as any outstanding athlete would receive. Let's make good character as important as athletic ability. *We're talking about an award to be given to one boy and one girl each year as the top award that any senior can receive.* Set the stage for something special, making sure there is a banquet or a time during graduation designed just to recognize these good citizens. The local media should be all over this event. You want every child in town to dream of being the student who receives the good-citizen scholarship.

If you handle it properly, you will probably find an outstanding citizen who deserves to have the scholarship named in his or her honor and will be capable of providing most of the money for the scholarship. When you develop guidelines similar to the ones below, churches, civic clubs, and businesses in your community will help you to provide a significant award for those young people who will become the next great generation. We let athletes have their day in the sun; why not let really good kids have theirs too?

Qualifications for the Good-Citizen Scholarship

1. Student must make good enough grades to have an opportunity to succeed in college. (If this criterion is met, higher grades are not to be considered as an advantage for one student over another.)
2. Student must have demonstrated good manners in all school activities.
3. Student must be able to demonstrate at least three service-oriented activities that he or she is involved in which help other people.
4. Student must have demonstrated dependability in a work environment.
5. Student must demonstrate kindness to all student populations, including those who are not considered a part of the in-crowd.
6. Student must be nominated by a teacher, administrator, or community leader.

7. Student must agree that after graduation he or she will contribute at least $100 per year to help support future students in the program.

SUMMARY

The stone of integrity we have just thrown into the water will now start the healing process for our nation. Our growing circles of moral influence will defeat the tidal wave of negative values.

We can start this ripple in the water by clearly defining the word "integrity." Integrity consists of three aspects: knowing the truth, acting on the truth, and letting others know that we are acting on that truth. If any of these components are absent, we may honestly believe that we are people of integrity, when, in fact we are only kidding ourselves.

Once we have defined integrity, we begin to develop it by incorporating common courtesy into our daily lives. This courteous behavior, coupled with respect for others and a positive attitude about life, will begin to change our character. As we change our behavior towards others, their attitudes will reflect our new approach to interaction. As the interaction between people becomes more civil, other positive personality traits will follow.

Integrity, as we will continue to learn in future chapters, will always depend on having the proper motivation and foundation. A person acquires integrity when he lives up to the standard that forms the foundation of his life. If we have a core of beliefs that come from God's eternal Word, and we live up to those beliefs, we become people of true integrity.

Obviously, these principles become meaningless if we are unwilling to stand up for what we believe. Many people understand the principles of right and wrong, but because of greed or some other character weakness, they are unwilling to live up to those principles. People of integrity will live up to their values, even if there are negative consequences. Integrity does not shift with the tide; it remains strong in all situations.

In order to build people of integrity, we must build community support by sponsoring scholarship programs for students who exhibit integrity. We must also be sure to support people of integrity in all public offices, from our school board representatives to our nationally elected officials.

STUDY GUIDE: CHAPTER 3
ENERGIZING PEOPLE OF INTEGRITY

I. Discuss the following passages:
   A. Proverbs 18:10: "The name of the Lord is a strong tower; the righteous run to it and are safe."
      1. If the Lord protects the righteous, why do we struggle with integrity?
      2. Why do you believe that righteous people can trust the Lord to protect them?
   B. Psalm 34:15–22
      1. How does the Lord protect the righteous?
      2. When have you seen evidence of the Lord's care for a righteous person?
      3. What does it mean that the memory of those who do evil will be cut off from the earth?
      4. What legacy does a righteous man or woman leave for the future generations?

II. Review the tidal wave of negative values and the reasons Americans lack integrity.

III. Do you agree with the three-part definition of integrity in this chapter?
   A. What do you think about the father who refused to allow his daughter to come home for visits while she lived with her boyfriend? Do you agree with his actions? Would there be a better way to maintain integrity and deal with the situation?
   B. Do you agree with the statement that when we refuse to stand up for the truth because we believe the battle is already lost, we lack integrity?
   C. Do you agree with the steps of moral development in children which are described in this chapter?
   D. What do you believe is the best way to impact character

development in your children?

IV. How can we can develop integrity?
   A. Do you agree that life's problems are very complex, but the solutions are simple? Why, or why not?
   B. Is the use of statements of respect, such as "Yes, sir," and "No, sir," really important?
   C. How important is the way children talk in the development of their overall moral values?
   D. How important is common courtesy?
   E. Do you agree with the author that attitudes change reality? Why, or why not?
   F. Why is inner motivation so important in our lives?
   G. What are the risks that a person must take in order to live a life of integrity?
   H. In what ways will the immoral minority control the minds of our children if we do not speak up for the truth?
   I. How can you build community support for good moral conduct in your city?

V. Building personal integrity:
   A. What are five things you will do to build respect in your home?
   B. Write down a plan of action to develop those concepts into habits in your home.
   C. What are five ways you will start to show respect for other people outside your home?
   D. What are the ways negative thoughts and values come into your home?
   E. How will you limit those negative thoughts and values?
   F. List the principles upon which you want every member of your family to build his or her life. (The fruit of the Spirit in Galatians 5:22, 23 and the Christian graces in II Peter 1:5–8 are good places to start your search.)
   G. Describe the ways you can make those principles a part of your daily life.
   H. List the ways you can help your community to encourage the development of these principles.

STEP TWO: RESTORING OUR FAMILIES

4
FOUR DAGGERS IN THE HEART OF THE AMERICAN FAMILY

Four disastrous developments have had a major impact on American homes in recent years. These daggers to the heart have shaken the very definition of marriage, while devastating millions of lives.

The first of these weapons against the family is the continued increase in the number of children who are being born to single, unwed parents. According to statistics, more and more children are being raised outside the bounds of a traditional home. Living without both parents automatically puts a child at a disadvantage in almost every area of life.

The second destructive weapon against the family is the prolific number of divorces in our society. Children from divorced parents often face as many struggles as those raised by unwed parents. The struggle can become even greater if the parents are at war with each other. The child will often grow up with a totally incorrect idea of family. With the pain of their parents' divorce embedded in their minds, these children often struggle to develop lasting relationships.

The third dagger is the increased pressure to accept homosexual marriage. As defined by God, marriage is a relationship between a man and a woman. (See Gen. 2:18–25.) With the increase of homosexual relationships, our country has also seen an increase in child abuse, spousal abuse, and sexual confusion among young people.

The fourth development that has had a major impact on American homes is the increased pressure to accept abortion. Despite what may seem an easy way out of a tough situation, research shows that the effects of abortion are traumatic and affect more than just the unborn child.

Satisfaction and success in life can generally be linked directly with the quality of a person's home life. In his book *The Future of the American Family,* George Barna states,

> The most impressive conclusion I've drawn from this research is that people believe that the health of our families is vitally important. Regardless of their particular inclinations or beliefs, the vast majority of Americans care about the family. And deep down in their hearts, they seem to know that as the family goes, so goes American society. The future of the family is not simply a matter of academic interest; it is an issue that touches directly on the well-being of American society itself.[1]

Barna also declares,

> Traditionally, one of the most important sources of stability has been our enduring faith in family. Despite the monumental social changes of recent times, we continue to maintain the belief that when all else fails, the family will be there to help pull us through. Regardless of whether that expectation is realistic or not, the peace of mind provided by such a notion still eases the anxiety of many Americans.[2]

Stability and peace of mind—these are great blessings never realized by many Americans because we have not protected the traditional family. How many people do you know who are in stable relationships, enjoying total peace of mind? Probably not very many. Knowing where you belong, knowing where you fit, knowing who will always be there with you and for you are concepts that lead to a lifetime of peace. We need the security,

---

[1] George Barna, *The Future of the American Family* (Chicago, Ill.: Moody Press, 1993), 19.
[2] Ibid., 18.

support, and love provided by a good solid home. The problem is that we can no longer define family.

On one occasion, a high school teacher asked me to share with her class the concepts I use in premarital counseling. After the class, she said bluntly, "Don't you know they have no idea what you are talking about? These students can't relate to the kind of love and commitment you talked about; 22 out of 23 of them come from broken homes." What an eye opener. Not only did I miss the mark, they didn't even have a reference point to understand the concept of a traditional, loving home.

Today there are four major threats facing our families: children being born outside the security of a loving home, negative effects of divorce on people, the efforts of homosexuals to change the structure of the family, and the devastating effects of abortion.

CHILDREN BEING BORN OUTSIDE THE SECURITY OF A LOVING HOME

Janice is pregnant; Her whole world has been turned upside down. Her boyfriend has decided he wants to date around. She now knows that he will not help raise the baby. The shock to her parents has been almost unbearable. They are ashamed, angry and confused. Their lives have also been turned upside down. They were looking forward to having the house to themselves, as Janice was the last child to graduate from high school. She was scheduled to attend college and become a nurse while they enjoyed some quiet time with each other. Now they are wondering, Who will raise this child? If Janice does, she limits her chances for an education and her nursing career.

The child will also strain her future relationships. Now that her boyfriend is gone, whom can she date? How many really good young men want to date a girl with a small child? How can she find the time to date? What if she ever does get married? How do you start a family when you already have a child? What about the child's biological father? Will he interfere with her future marriage? What about adoption? If the child is adopted, will he or she have a good home? What if the adoptive parents are not good parents? How can you ever explain to a child that you gave him or her away?

On the other hand, how can Janice's parents raise the child? They are over fifty years old! When this child graduates from high school, they will be past retirement age! What are the good options? Are there any good options? Maybe all of this should have been discussed before Janice became sexually active!

Janice decided to keep the baby. Her boyfriend, who was the classically irresponsible teenage stud, began having sexual relations with another girl. Shortly before Janice's baby girl was born, they discovered that his new girlfriend was also expecting a child. There would be no help from him as she raises this beautiful, innocent, little girl. Janice is now torn with emotion, a hatred for the unfaithful boyfriend, a love for the precious little baby, and a constant battle with the guilt of the whole situation.

Her parents are also struggling with the radical changes in their lives. They want to love the child, but that love is mingled with total disdain for the baby's father. Their disappointment in their daughter shows in everyday attitudes toward her and the child. They are helpful, but more distant than before in their relationship with Janice. Janice's father is struggling to figure out the financial needs of his now enlarged family, while her mother tries to balance her work schedule with the needs of her daughter and granddaughter. She is also battling with bitterness over the loss of her life's plans and the loss of her daughter's future.

This is no longer a happy home! Why don't we spend time telling young people the truth about sexual activity and its possible outcome? Can't we work into our sex education courses at school a little study of the emotional effects of lifetime choices? In fact, maybe some of you educators should develop a course, not on sex education, but on "Making Lifetime Choices," including sexual activity, marriage, college and career choices, health choices, and other important lifetime decisions.

As a result of a bad decision, there is one more child to be included in the ever-increasing number of children who are reared by unmarried parents. Between 1983 and 1993, births to unmarried women increased 70 percent to 6.3 million children!

That means 27 percent of all children live with single, never-married parents. Before 1983, only 3.7 million children were in that situation, while in 1963 there were only 243,000.[3] Think about it: One-fourth of all children never have the chance to live with a mommy and a daddy who show them how to love another person. The majority of these children were being raised by their mothers, without the aid of a loving father.

There are three major negative effects on the next generation when the father is not a part of the family unit. First, if there is not a proper relationship with a father, there will be problems in the normal development of gender roles. It has been discovered that a positive relationship with a father has a great impact on the development of masculinity in males and femininity in females.[4] Second, there is a direct correlation between the closeness of children's relationships with their fathers and the way they develop their moral standards.[5] The third problem is academic performance. A warm father-child relationship has a definite positive effect on a child's ability and desire to learn. The lack of development in cognitive skills is especially pronounced in young boys. The relationship of a father and a son has a great impact on the accomplishments of that boy in school.[6]

Recently, I sat in a room with a young man from a broken home, twenty years old, a high-school dropout, sitting next to his nineteen-year-old girlfriend, also a high-school dropout. They are expecting a child. We talked about supporting the child financially, and the young man responded by saying he didn't have a job, but he thought he could get one at a fast food restaurant. We talked about where they would live. He had no idea of where to live or even the cost of an apartment. We talked about future plans, and the pair had none. Because of a lack of training at home,

---

[3]Gary R. Collins, *Family Shock* (Wheaton, Ill.: Tyndale House Publisher, 1995), 90.
[4]Michael E. Lamb, *The Role of the Father in Child Development* (Hoboken, N.J.: John Wiley & Sons, 2004), 5.
[5]Ibid., 11.
[6]Ibid., 8.

this young couple is already in big trouble, and the bigger problem is that they don't even understand why.

In his book *Nurturing a Child's Soul,* Timothy K. Jones states, "I'm convinced that just being there is half the battle of parenting. Parenting is a contact sport; we show up. We engage our children's eyes. We hold them, hug them, pat them, and rub shoulders with them."[7] When young people see the model of loving parents, they have the opportunity to learn about life. They may not be perfectly prepared for marriage or the responsibility of rearing children, but at least they will have a picture of what can be. When one parent is absent, the education level goes down, the ability to form relationships is impaired, and the hope of a future grows dim.

THE NEGATIVE EFFECTS OF DIVORCE ON OUR PEOPLE

While births to unwed mothers are a serious challenge to our culture, they are not our only problem. At some point in their lives, before the age of eighteen, 2 out of 3 children born this year will live in a single-parent household.[8] Although unwed mothers pose a problem, divorce constitutes an even bigger hazard for the next generation. Unless we are able to keep families together, we will never develop another "Greatest Generation" because divorce has a *lifetime* effect on children. In a twenty-eight-year study of children reared by divorced parents, Judith S. Wallerstein and her fellow researchers came to this conclusion:

> Divorce is a life-transforming experience. After divorce, childhood is different. Adolescence is different. Adulthood—with the decision to marry or not and have children or not—is different. Whether the final outcome is

---

[7]Timothy K. Jones, *Nurturing a Child's Soul* (Nashville, Tenn.: Word Publishing, 2000), 42.
[8]Barna, 23.

good or bad, the whole trajectory of an individual's life is profoundly altered by the divorce experience.[9]

Please understand that the following conclusions are drawn from society as a whole. It does not mean that these characteristics will apply in every situation. There are a number of very loving, caring people who have suffered the trauma of divorce, but have still been able to rear good, successful children. The problem is that the odds are against them. It is a tremendous uphill struggle. Consider the following problems faced by the children of divorced parents.

The Immediate Impact on the Children
Children from divorced families often lose their childhood. Because the parents are struggling with the loss of their marital relationship, they often become dependant on the children for comfort and care. The child is now the adult, often taking on the roles of counselor for the parent, caretaker of smaller children, and housekeeper. These children lose the carefree play of youth as well as the comforting arms and lap of a loving parent—who is now always rushing off because life in the post-divorce family is incredibly difficult to manage.[10]

As if it were not bad enough to have one parent depending on his or her children for strength, many children in a divorce will lose the other parent entirely. As life progresses, the parent who does not have the majority of the childcare responsibilities will become less and less involved in the child's life. Although the child still loves the parent and wants a relationship with that parent, there is never enough time or money for that parent to be truly a part of his or her life. They simply move on in another direction, starting a new life with a new family, while the child is left feeling emotionally drained and abandoned.

Life also becomes more stressful, as divorce often results in many changes in children's living situations such as changing

---

[9]Judith S. Wallerstein, Julia M. Lewis, and Sandra Blakeslee, *The Unexpected Legacy of Divorce* (New York: Hyperion Books, 2000), xxvii.
[10]Ibid., 296.

schools, child-care centers, homes, etc. Relationships with friends and extended family members are affected as the child is forced to adjust to the new lifestyle of the parents, who are adjusting to new friends and strained family relationships. For the child, there is no real choice. They must adjust everything in their lives to coincide with the new lives of their parents. The stress can be overpowering.

The Effects of Poor Parental Adjustment on the Children
It is generally agreed that the manner in which children fare in families is due in part to the mental health of the parents. When parents are struggling with the issues associated with divorce, they will very often battle with depression and other emotional problems. These struggles, in turn, affect the emotional health of children. It is difficult for a child to understand why his or her mother is crying when she goes to bed at night. It is hard for a child to understand why his or her father is angry all the time. The natural tendency of a child is to think that he or she has caused the parents' distress, and the child will tend to become just as moody and maladjusted as the parent.

The Effects of a Lack of Parental Competence on the Children
Almost everything that happens to a child is affected by the parenting skills of both parents. Since one parent is absent and both parents are often fighting with each other, little time is devoted to developing proper parenting skills. Time to play games, do homework, or just to talk is no longer a priority for the struggling parent. They are often so occupied with surviving that little time is left for good discipline or proper interaction with children. Parenting has now changed from training the children to passing the children back and forth, with each parent trying to influence the children to love him or her more than the other parent. Many parents become more interested in bribing the child with gifts than in training and disciplining the child properly. The incompetence of parents following a divorce is likely to have considerable influence on how the children are doing.

The Children's Exposure to Interparental Conflict

Conflict is frequently part of family dynamics and may be especially common in families that have undergone divorce. The degree to which children are exposed to conflict will have a substantial effect on the children's well-being. Children want to love both parents; yet, when the parents are continuously arguing or criticizing each other, the child is forced to listen as terrible things are said about the two people he or she loves the most.[11]

Difficulties in All Areas of Development

Researchers have found significant differences in learning problems, school dropout rates, early sexual behavior, physical illnesses, anger towards parents, and a host of other very important social measures in connection with divorced parents. In other words, every aspect of a child's life is affected by the radical changes in the lives of the parents. A young person will react to every situation differently because the foundation of his or her thought processes has been uprooted.[12]

Struggles as Adults

The struggle of children reared in a home divided by divorce does not end when they leave home. Researchers have discovered that the trauma caused by the loss of a home continues throughout life. The first way the trauma of divorce affects an adult who grew up in a divorced family is the development of what is called "the terror of conflict." According to Wallerstein,[13] even when they are in very loving relationships, adult children of divorce often have great fears every time there is a normal conflict in their own marriage. Since the only model of conflict resolution they have seen is for one party to leave, they have an unreasonable fear that their loving mate will leave them at the first sign of conflict. Because the divorce that broke up their home ended their carefree, happy childhood, many adults from divorced families have great difficulty enjoying the good

---

[11]Ibid., 15.
[12]Ibid.
[13]Ibid.

times in life. As a result of previous events in their lives, they are always waiting for the other shoe to drop. Their line of thought is, "If things are good, there must be something bad just around the corner."

We will be unable to restore the upward movement of our society if we do not implement training, counseling, and even laws which help adults to understand their responsibilities to the children they bring into the world. S. Coopersmith observes,

> We talk about the deleterious effect of divorce on children, but in a society that has come to value the individual's freedom above the individual's commitments, we too often lack the integrity to transform our talk into action. So let us be very clear: The responsibility of parents to do what is best for their children is a moral absolute. Those who are not willing to carry out this duty should never bring children into the world.[14]

THE EFFORTS OF HOMOSEXUALS TO CHANGE THE STRUCTURE OF THE FAMILY

On the outside, Bob looked like the classic success story. He was a recent college graduate with a master's degree. A fine athlete who married his college sweetheart, landed a great job, bought a home, and was seemingly off to a great start. However, the nightmares never stopped; they were dark, disturbing pictures. The dreams always had dark forces chasing him. Sometime those forces hurt him; other times those forces caused him to hurt others. He had a growing desire for pornography and even started driving to areas known for prostitution. He found himself longing for the ugly, dirty side of life.

At times his anger became so strong he was both verbally and physically abusive toward his wife. Eventually, she had to get a restraining order against Bob. His work suffered to the

---

[14]S. Coopersmith, "Self-Concept Research Implications for Education," Paper presented to the American Education Research Association, Los Angeles, California, 6 February 1929, 142.

point he could no longer hold a job. He had now gone from a great success in life to a total wreck, with a wife who loved him but couldn't live with him, and no job.

When he finally got help, he was able to release the anger that was destroying his life. Bob had been raped by a man he trusted when he was eight years old. The scars had built up to the point that he could no longer live with the shame. Fortunately, over a year's time, with counseling and serious Bible study, Bob was able to reclaim his life. Make no mistake about it: Lives are being destroyed by homosexual predators.

The third major attack on our families comes from the attempts by homosexuals to have their lifestyle accepted as a form of marriage. The American people are being deceived into believing that homosexuality is just another harmless lifestyle when in reality it is a *perversion* of God's most precious creation, human beings. "So God created man in his own image, in the image of God he created him; male and female he created them" (Gen. 1:27). If we are to restore the upward movement of our nation, we must realize that any movement back to a unisex lifestyle is a movement *downward*.

When the homosexual lifestyle is examined, that downward movement becomes apparent in several ways. First, the homosexual lifestyle is dangerous to children. It's a fact that homosexuals put our children at greater risk of being sexually abused. Consider the statistics: While approximately 2 percent of the people in the US are homosexual (US census 2000), almost 30 percent of all sexual abuse is homosexual in nature.

While heterosexuals outnumber homosexuals by a ratio of 50 to 1, homosexual pedophiles commit about 1 out of 3 sexual offenses.[15]

During the sexual abuse scandal in the Catholic Church, the news media, obviously trying to protect homosexuals, refused to report that the abuse was males abusing males. In his book

---

[15]Marie E. Tomeo, Donald Templer, Susan Anderson, and Debra Kotler, "Comparative Data of Childhood and Adolescence Molestation in Heterosexual and Homosexual Persons," *Archives of Sexual Behavior* 30 (October 2001), 539.

The Courage to be Catholic, George Weigel cites 285 cases of child abuse. The sex of those abused by priests is listed in 151 of those cases. A priest sexually assaulted a girl in only one of those cases. In 150 of the 151 cases listed, priests assaulted boys. That is *homosexual abuse*.[16]

The number of sexual abuse cases per capita involving homosexuals outnumbers heterosexual abuse cases 20 to 1!

It is often a response to same-sex abuse that causes an adult to "choose" the homosexual lifestyle and possibly become a pedophile. According to Dr. David Finkelhor, 46 percent of homosexual men and 22 percent of homosexual women reported having been molested by a person of the same gender, while only 7 percent of heterosexual men report having been molested, and only 1 percent of heterosexual women report having been molested by a person of the opposite gender.[17] Dr. David Finkelhor also reports that "boys victimized by older men were over four times more likely to be presently involved in homosexual activity than are non-victims."[18]

The possibility of pedophilia is not the only danger involved with the homosexual lifestyle. According to statistics supplied by the Federal Bureau of Investigation and homosexual activists themselves, homosexual couples are far more violent than married heterosexuals and have shorter life spans due to their more dangerous lifestyles. According to the FBI, there were only 1,317 so-called "hate crimes" against homosexuals in 1999—nearly half of which were name-calling. Meanwhile, homosexual activists and authors David Island and Patrick Letellier report that as many as 500,000 men are victims of domestic violence at the hands of their homosexual sex partners. In their book *Men Who Beat the Men Who Love Them*, Island and Letellier write, "The

---

[16]George Weigel, *The Courage to be Catholic* (New York: Basic Books, 2002), 9-20.
[17]Tomeo, 539.
[18]Ibid.

probability of violence occurring in a gay couple is mathematically double the probability of that in a heterosexual couple." Island and Letellier also estimate, "domestic violence may affect and poison as many as 50 percent of gay male couples," while "we believe [heterosexual domestic abuse] is closer to 20 percent."[19]

According to the Community United Against Violence, a homosexual group that combats domestic violence in the homosexual community, "The truth of the matter is, however, that you are much more likely to be injured by someone you love than by a gay-basher on the street." Gary Glenn writes, "So the homosexual activists themselves admit that homosexual couples are much more dangerous and, hence, unsuitable for raising children."[20]

Now consider how difficult the teenage years would be for a child adopted by homosexual parents. Keep in mind that 98 percent of all children are heterosexual, but this child is being raised watching his or her mother kiss his or her other mother or his or her father kiss his or her other father. Understanding sexual relationships can be difficult for young people under any circumstances, but what will this young person become?

In our country today, we must find a way to encourage young men to be men and not turn to homosexual activity or become feminine in their thinking. There has been much writing in the past few years about men "getting in touch" with their feminine side. Personally, my feminine side is on a slow boat headed for China. I don't want to think like a woman any more than I want my wife to think like a man. Don't misunderstand what I am saying: Being macho, harsh, or hateful is not being manly! Males should always be gentlemen who understand how to treat women with respect, as they maintain their competitive and protective nature. We must always remember that men and women

---

[19]David Island and Patrick Letillier, *Men Who Beat the Men Who Love Them* (Binghamton, N.Y.: Haworth Press, 1991), 14, 15.
[20]Gary Glenn, "Family group tells task force: real threat of violence against homosexuals is attack by their own sex partners," *AFA Michigan* (15 March 2001).

are created differently and have different emotions, thought processes, and physical appearances. Without trying to place one above the other, we should honor these differences.

THE DEVASTATING EFFECTS OF ABORTION

Kim sat with her mother and father in the middle of the auditorium as the preacher delivered a remarkable message about the love and grace of God, but she never lifted her head to look in his direction. Her eyes had lost all their sparkle; her friendly, warm smile was nowhere to be seen. Her mother tried to put her arm around Kim's shoulder, but Kim pushed it away. Tears streamed down her cheeks. Unknown to her parents, a few days earlier, pressure from her boyfriend had influenced her into an ill-fated trip to an abortion clinic. Now sitting in church, the grief and shame hid the message of grace from her crying eyes. She knew she had taken the life of her unborn child. Her body still felt the changes caused by the pregnancy. Her thoughts drifted to scenes of a child growing up in the loving arms of her mother. In her mind, she saw the little dresses she would buy for her baby girl. She envisioned the first steps and the first words. All dreams that would never happen! The child would never see the light of its first morning.

A few days later, the preacher received a desperate call from Kim's father, "Please help us! Kim is in trouble!" "What's the problem?" the preacher asked. "She is really depressed; we found a note in her room written to God," the father explained. He continued, "She is so depressed, I think she may commit suicide. She had an abortion; now we don't know what to do."

With counseling and the loving help of her family, Kim is no longer considering suicide; however, she is left with a knife wound in her soul which will always remain. She will forever live with the result of her decisions. Sex outside of marriage, that's easy. Having an abortion, that's not so easy. Living with the fact that she has destroyed a life is almost impossible. [21]

---

[21]Adapted from Jayne E. Schooler, *Mom, Dad . . . I'm Pregnant* (Colorado Springs, Colo.: NavPress, 2004), 21–25.

FOUR DAGGERS IN THE HEART OF THE AMERICAN FAMILY

Similar family crises are being repeated every day in our country. Girls feel forced to accept the only way they know to get out of a terrible situation. They elect to end the life of a child which is growing in their bodies. Why would anyone make such a choice? Jayne E. Schooler explains some of the reasons in her book, *Mom, Dad . . . I'm Pregnant*:

1. Threat of the loss of a college education.
2. Threat of rejection by parents and boyfriend.
3. Threat of financial insecurity.
4. Threat of the loss of a lifestyle she has known.
5. Threat of the loss of respect and reputation if the pregnancy is known.[22]

All of those fears are real! If she had the baby, she would have faced all of these consequences. However, now that she has elected to have an abortion, she must endure an equally harsh set of realities.

It is true that sexual activity is enjoyable and young people find pleasure in fulfilling their physical needs—but at what price? There is always the possibility of an unexpected and unwanted pregnancy, which will change the person's life forever. They should understand that no birth control method other than abstinence is 100 percent safe.

Although many young people have decided that abortion is an easy way out of the dilemma caused by unexpected pregnancy, the emotional scars will continue for a lifetime. Although Planned Parenthood and other groups supporting abortion rights for women continue to claim that there are no harmful emotional effects caused by abortions, please consider the following research findings:

A five-year retrospective study in two Canadian provinces found significantly greater use of medical and psychiatric services among women who had abortions. Most significant was the finding that 25 percent of women who had an abortion made visits to psychiatrists as compared to 3 percent of those who

---

[22]Ibid., 86.

had never received an abortion.[23] There are a number of reported detrimental emotional responses to abortions. Whether the abortion was by choice or provoked by a medical need, some of the following emotional responses may occur.

Post-Traumatic Stress Disorder

A study by Catherine Barnard in 1990 found that a minimum of 19 percent of the women who received an abortion would suffer some, if not all, of the effects of post-traumatic stress disorder. This disorder results in feelings of intense fear, feelings of helplessness or being trapped, and a loss of emotional control.[24]

Sexual Dysfunction

Research also indicates that 30 to 50 percent of women who have an abortion report experiencing sexual dysfunctions, beginning immediately after their abortions.[25]

Increase in Suicide Attempts

The suicide rate within one year after an abortion is three times higher than for all women, seven times higher than for women carrying their baby to term, and nearly twice as high as the rate for women who suffered a miscarriage. Suicide attempts are especially prevalent among post-abortion teenagers.[26]

Other Documented Negative Health Effects

Increased alcohol abuse, increased drug abuse, eating disorders, and increased problems in marriage have also been linked to the emotional effects of abortion. To study more on these topics, see the works listed in the bibliography.

---

[23]Wallerstein, Lewis, and Blakeslee, 313–21.

[24]Catherine Barnard, *The Long-Term Psychological Effects of Abortion* (Portsmouth, N.H.: Institute for Pregnancy Loss, 1990).

[25]Anne Speckhard and Vincent M. Rue, "Postabortion Syndrome: An emerging public health concern," *Journal of Social Issues*, 48 (Fall 1992): 95–119.

[26]Ibid.

FOUR DAGGERS IN THE HEART OF THE AMERICAN FAMILY

SUMMARY

As we have noted, four major attacks are being launched against our homes, beginning with the large number of women who are having children outside of marriage. Children without both parents generally experience major adjustment problems in their lives. Without a father figure in the home, the development of masculine or feminine characters is confused. It has also been demonstrated that a child's relationship with his or her father has a direct impact on the development of moral character. Third, academics usually suffer when both parents are not available to help.

The second major impact on our families comes from the consistently high number of divorces in our country. Children from the homes of divorced parents will always carry with them some scars from their childhood. These painful experiences result in lifelong problems. As children lose the security of their childhood, they must also deal with the struggle experienced by the parents. As parents fight with each other and try to establish their own new lives, the child becomes more of a parent than a child. These early struggles will result in the loss of childhood development as well as the joys of childhood.

The third attack on a good home environment comes from the homosexual community. Homosexuality is not a harmless lifestyle to be tolerated by everyone. The homosexual lifestyle carries with it an increase in child abuse, an increase in domestic violence, and an increase in the AIDS epidemic. It is time for Americans to address these issues honestly. Christians must start asking for hard, honest answers. The homosexual movement continues to change our view of the family, as they push for more and more rights. However, child abuse, confusion, and the decline of our nation can be seen as the end result of this movement.

Abortion has also left a huge scar in the fabric of our homes. When an abortion takes place a life is lost, and a family suffers. The expectant mother suffers the guilt of her action, and the rest of her family struggles to understand the change in her attitude about life.

STUDY GUIDE: CHAPTER 4
FOUR DAGGERS IN THE HEART
OF THE AMERICAN FAMILY

I. Consider the following passages:
   A. Malachi 2:16; Matthew 19:4–12
      1. What is God's attitude toward divorce?
      2. What are the reasons people get divorced?
      3. Are those reasons acceptable to God?
      4. According to the Bible, what reasons are acceptable to God for divorce?
   B. Romans 1:24–27; I Corinthians 6:9–11
      1. What words does Paul use to describe homosexual relationships?
      2. Do you agree with his statements? Why or why not?
      3. Do you believe that homosexuals will be lost?
      4. Can a person who has homosexual tendencies live a celibate life and be acceptable to God?

II. Review the lessons on integrity.

III. How powerful are the four major dangers facing the American home?
   A. Why is the home such an important part of the satisfaction a person gets out of life?
   B. What problems are developing in our society as a result of babies being born to unwed mothers?
   C. What are some of the problems which children face when they do not have a father figure in the home?
   D. Discuss the problems faced by children who come from divorced families.
   E. Discuss ways your class can help divorced parents as they try to rear good children.
   F. Discuss the lasting effects of divorce on adults who were raised in those families.
   G. What effects do you believe homosexual "families" have on our society?

FOUR DAGGERS IN THE HEART OF THE AMERICAN FAMILY

    H. Discuss the effects that abortion has on a woman who has had an abortion.
    I. Discuss the effects that an abortion has on relationships within a family.

IV. Personal action:
    A. Discuss these four major problems with your family.
    B. Share the facts in this chapter with your friends and family.
    C. Brainstorm with members of your church concerning ways you can address these problems in your community.
    D. Start classes in your church to teach decision-making in a way that will help young people understand the lasting effects of their decisions.

5
REBUILDING THE FAMILY OF THE AMERICAN DREAM

What life do you want for your children? The one described in the last chapter or a life with a loving family?

A father tells about a great day in the life of his son. Returning home after dark one beautiful day, he found his youngest son playing G.I. Joe with his best friend. The two had romped and played for hours, having great fun.

Dad dragged into the house just before bedtime, picked up his happy little boy, and told him he was a champion. He then bounced him like a basketball in the bed two or three times. He helped him brush his teeth and put on his pajamas, and then he tucked him into bed.

As he tucked the boy into bed, the father asked, "What was the highlight of your day today, Son?" The boy looked straight in the eyes of his father and said, "Getting bounced in the bed."

"Really?" responded the surprised father. "Why?"

"'Cause you were there, Daddy.... 'Cause you were there!"

The wise people of our day tell us that the Cleavers from the old TV show *Leave It to Beaver* don't live here anymore. The question is, Why not? We can still have great loving families. Listen to this mealtime exchange:

> "Jerry, how did your day go?"
> "Pretty good, Mom. I made a basket during our first basketball practice."
> "That's great, Son. Anything else happening?"
> "Reading test was a little hard, but I think I did okay. I'm sure looking forward to our camping trip this weekend, aren't you, Dad?"
> "Absolutely, but you know I have to finish up some

work on Saturday, so we won't be able to leave until about noon."

"That's okay. Mom and I need to get my fishing rod ready because you know I'll catch the biggest fish."

"I don't think so. Last time it was Mom who out-fished both of us."

This is a simple conversation about making memories for a lifetime. A family together, enjoying one another, is a great blessing! Recently, I talked with a forty-six-year-old woman who had just lost her dad to cancer. The tears were real, but so was the laughter as she recalled walks in the park as a small girl holding his hand. She remembered days when he picked her up from school for a special lunch. An especially important time was when she was in her thirties and was diagnosed with cancer. It was her dad who took her to every one of her radiation treatments. It was her mother, father, and husband who became her greatest cheerleaders as she won the battle and is now cancer free. This family knows it will never really lose its father. He will always be alive in their hearts, and he will be waiting patiently for them in heaven. What a blessing! The Cleavers can live in twenty-first-century America if we will invest our lives in our families.

The burning question is, How? How can we restore the warmth and love of traditional family life? The restoration of families begins with a lifetime commitment to total fidelity and integrity in marriage.

BUILDING INTEGRITY AND FIDELITY IN OUR HOMES

Our search for solutions to the problems of our homes begins with the very simple concept of restoring purity and fidelity in marriage. The foundation of our society is the home, and the foundation of a home is the commitment of one man to one woman for life. By re-establishing the biblical principles of purity before marriage and fidelity in marriage, we can build homes filled with love and purpose.

In this age of immediate gratification, we must ask, "Why would our children accept such an outdated concept?" As we have noted, morals are taught and role models are developed at an early age, so if we begin to teach children at a young age, the result will be a lifestyle of faithfulness to one person. Consider all the pain young people allow into their lives when they choose an immoral lifestyle.

The lifestyle they are embracing inevitably leads to a loss of self-esteem. Young people often have difficulty understanding the way a loss of self-esteem inevitably follows the breakup of an intimate relationship. Teenagers who accept a permissive approach to sexual relationships are opening themselves up to associations with people who have no desire for a permanent commitment. When one person thinks he or she is in love and the other is just having a good time, the result has a disastrous effect on an individual's self-worth. An intimate relationship with a member of the opposite sex always causes a deep emotional bond; if the relationship is broken, there will be a lasting negative impact on the people involved.

I once worked with a fine young man who had a beautiful Christian wife and a wonderful baby boy. From the outside it looked like the perfect Christian home. However, before he started to date his wife, he had lived an immoral lifestyle. Once he confessed to me that he was having trouble in his relationship with his wife because every time they made love, he saw the faces of the girls he had been with before he was married. The emotional strain became too great for him, and he eventually left his wife and child behind to live without the blessings of their love. It was devastating to this fine young woman and her little boy. For the rest of their lives, they will suffer because of the early transgressions of this man.

The lifestyle they are accepting ultimately leads to loneliness. The one who lives an immoral lifestyle will know the loneliness of having a partner who does not love him or is not totally devoted to him. Our young people need to understand the long-term effects of decisions about love and commitment. It is extremely sad to see a person who is fifty or sixty years old living by himself or herself without the blessings of a loving family.

Many of these people have had a number of sexual partners, marriages, and often several children. However, because of their choice for instant gratification rather than a long-term commitment of love, they are now alone and have little or no contact with children or family.

As we get older, more and more of the very satisfying experiences of life come from those people in our family who love us. By choosing to shift from one relationship to another, our children will miss the opportunity to rear their children in an environment encircled by the love of an entire family.

On the other hand, consider what those who choose a lifelong commitment will enjoy:

Those who choose a lifetime commitment will know the beauty of a relationship where two people know they have given themselves to each other for a lifetime of love. Although young love is exciting, it lacks the power and satisfaction of the lifetime of shared love. Two people who live side by side, experiencing the joys of raising little children, share the most satisfying love. This love grows as they guide their children though teenage years and watch them eventually start their own families. Together they share the joys of holidays with the family, as well as the excitement of buying a home together, considering retirement together, traveling together, and caring for each other year after year.

The love of a committed marriage also grows when the stress of illness is shared with a loving mate. Two people who are committed to each other for life will help each other through the shared pain of the loss of aging parents, along with the daily stress of financial and career struggles. As one writer has correctly said, "A joy shared is twice the joy, a sorrow shared is half the sorrow." Those who select a lifetime with one person know the security of trusting one person with complete confidence in all situations.

One of the greatest joys in life can only be experienced by a husband and a wife who have made a complete, lifetime commitment to each other. It is the security of knowing that they will always be faithful to each other. There is a confident peace of mind that those who select other lifestyles will never experience. Although security is an under-used word in our society, it is a great blessing to those who have the security and comfort of knowing exactly where they belong and with whom they will spend their entire lives.

Those who select morally pure lives with a permanent commitment to their mates will also experience a special relationship with their children. They will have the opportunity to experience a relationship with children who marvel at their parents' love, devotion, and faithfulness. As that respect grows, the aging parents will be able to see their children grow up to have great homes of their own.

You can learn a tremendous amount about a person by preparing his or her funeral. It is my custom to meet with the family before the funeral and listen as they share their memories of the loved one who has died. When Johnny's wife and four grown daughters gathered to tell about his life, it was more like preparation for a party than a funeral. Johnny's wife of fifty-three years smiled and quietly told about his patience and love. Each of the four daughters told of special times with their father, and each one laughed as they told of the special jokes they shared with their father. We spent an entire afternoon laughing as we talked about a very special man who had left a powerful legacy of love for his family.

Those who opt for a life of faithfulness will be able to enjoy growing old together with no regrets. There is no need to look back on life with regrets or guilt. They have loved each other and loved their children. Together the couple walks hand in hand into the sunset years of life. They laugh about the good times and remember the hard times with the pride of two people who helped each other overcome. This couple is able to enjoy holidays and special events with their children and grandchildren as love radiates throughout their family. Their fifty-year wedding anniversary celebration is a reminder of the great life they have shared as one.

Look at the impact their lives will have on the rest of their family as they have set a pattern of love and commitment for each member of the family to follow.

Which lifestyle do you want for your children?

There is a reason why Jesus told His disciples that marriage was a permanent relationship in Matthew 19:4–6. "Haven't you read," He replied, "that at the beginning the Creator made them male and female, and said, 'For this reason a man will leave his father and mother and be united to his wife, and the two will become one flesh?' So they are no longer two, but one. Therefore what God has joined together, let man not separate."

The following four characteristics will build lasting homes and provide a foundation for the future of our children.

1. Total Fidelity

Marriage is a civilizing institution, a means of curbing desires or inclinations that might otherwise make social stability impossible. The device through which marriage performs this crucial function is the notion of fidelity.[1] We must model for our children "total fidelity."

While many people think of fidelity as faithfulness in sexual relationships, true faithfulness encompasses much more. Our children need to see mothers and fathers who really fulfill the vows they made before God when they were married. Do you remember those vows? "Will you love, honor and cherish one another, in sickness and in health, for better or for worse, for richer or for poorer, and forsaking all others keep yourself to him (or her) and him (or her) alone as long as you both shall live?"

Our children need *to see* parents who really honor each other, parents who speak to each other with kindness and courtesy, parents who nourish their love daily with soft words and kind actions. Real fidelity in marriage is not just remaining sexually faithful. It is being faithful by loving and honoring your mate.

You can get a good reminder of what fidelity and love in a marriage means by reading out loud I Corinthians 13. As you read, put your name and your mate's name into each phrase as the characteristics of love are described. When you do, it will sound something like this:

---

[1]Steven Carter, *Integrity* (New York: Harper/Collins Publishers, 1996), 127.

If I, _____, speak in the tongues of men and of angels, but do not have _____'s love, I am only a resounding gong or a clanging cymbal. If I have the gift of prophecy and can fathom all mysteries and all knowledge, and if I have a faith that can move mountains, but do not have a love for _____, I am nothing. If I give all my possessions to the poor and surrender my body to the flames, but have not shared love with _____, I gain nothing. My love for _____ makes me patient at all times. My love for _____ is always kind. Because I love _____ I will not envy, boast, or be proud. My love for _____ will never be rude, nor is it self-seeking. Because I, _____, love _____, I am not easily angered, nor will I keep a record of wrongs. My love does not delight in evil but rejoices with the truth. My love for _____ will always protect him/her, trust him/her, and I will always share my hopes with him/her and will always persevere. My love for _____ will never fail.

If you will read that out loud and then write it down on paper, it will cause you to think of the kind of love you should share with your mate and the kind of example you should set for your children. After all, isn't that the type of loving relationship you want for your children?

2. Living with Purpose

Living with purpose is the second step in restoring the strength of the American family.

Have you ever taken the time to analyze the real values and goals of each member of your family? The families of the "Greatest Generation" were strong because they saw themselves as a part of something valuable and worthwhile. We should ask ourselves, "How is our family going to make an impact on this world? Whose life will be better because they came into contact with our family?"

Over twenty years ago, I sat down and developed a mission statement for my life, which has been a continuous direction and guiding force for me. Many times over the years, I have evaluated opportunities in light of that mission statement. If the opportunity didn't fit the goals I had outlined, I moved on to the next possibility. It has been that three-part mission statement that has motivated my prayers, my work, my interaction with people, and my family life over the years. You would be providing a great service to your family by sitting down with your mate and children to develop a mission statement for your family. In order to achieve a meaningful purpose for your family, ask each member of your family the following questions:

1. What will I do that will make life better for my family?
2. What will I do with my life that uses my talents to bless the lives of those in our community?
3. What will I do that makes the next generation better?
4. How will I help my family know God and have eternal life?
5. When my life is over, what will they say about me at the funeral?
6. When I meet God, will He be pleased with the way I used the gifts He gave to me?

The last question is the most important because God made each of us for a reason. Paul said it best: "For he chose us in him before the creation of the world to be holy and blameless in his sight" (Eph. 1:4). Think about it: Before the creation of the world, God knew who you were going to be, He knew your name, He knew if you were going to be male or female, and He had a purpose for your life! You were not created by accident; God intended to use you in His eternal plan. Now it's up to you to plan your life so He can use you for the good of the rest of His creation.

By the way, if you are worried about your children's self-esteem, just teach them that God knows them and that He needs them to complete His purposes on this earth. If they know God wants them, they will have the confidence to become the leaders of the next great generation.

3. Live with Joy

Living with a lifetime commitment and an eternal purpose can seem difficult if we don't apply the third principle of building our homes. Live with joy! Paul said, "Rejoice in the Lord always. I will say it again: Rejoice!" (Phil. 4:4).

If God gives you a day, you ought to enjoy it.

It is amazing to see how many people live each day as if it is going to be another terrible day. Why not enjoy the day? It's going to happen whether you are happy or sad; therefore, I'll choose to be happy.

When I am checking out at a store, I make it a habit to ask the clerk how his or her day is going, and it's a shame that so many have something negative to say: "Okay, for a Monday"; "I'd be doing fine if I didn't have to work"; "Oh, I just don't feel well today." I'm sure you've heard those gripes and hundreds of other daily complaints people make.

However, when I get ready to leave, they almost always say, "Have a nice day." That's my opportunity to change his or her thinking, so I respond, "I always do. Is there any other kind?" or, "I have a good day every day; I sure wouldn't want to waste one on a bad day," or, "If God gives us a day, we ought to enjoy it." I've discovered over the years that some clerks look forward to waiting on me because they really want to see the good side of life.

Your family needs to see the good side of life! I really believe that families have some great reasons to rejoice.

Rejoice in the love and trust of your mate. I know that your mate is not perfect, but what a great blessing it is to have someone who has devoted his or her life to loving you. Take the time to write down all the ways your mate has blessed your life. Remember to include holidays and vacations, and some of your special moments together. It doesn't matter if you are rich or poor, young or old, or even if you are healthy or sick, if you have someone who really loves you, you are blessed.

Two are better than one, because they have a good return

for their work: If one falls down, his friend can help him up. But pity the man who falls and has no one to help him up! Also, if two lie down together, they will keep warm. But how can one keep warm alone? (Eccles. 4:9–11).

Rejoice in the lives of your children. Children are not a battle or a curse; they are a blessing and a gift from God. Watch them grow up, and enjoy every minute of it. What in the world could be better than seeing your children play a ball game, or act in a silly school play, or perform in the band? What could be better than hugging them and praising them when they come home? Invest your time in the lives of your children, and you will have memories that last forever.

Speaking of great memories, on my daughter's first Christmas, she wasn't interested in the gifts, but she thought she should eat some of the wrapping paper. When the paper got stuck in her throat, Karen and I panicked! We grabbed the baby and our four-year-old son and rushed to the car. Karen was holding the baby in the front seat as I drove as fast as possible toward the hospital. Karen was scared and crying when this little hand from the back seat began to pat her shoulder, and our son calmly assured his mother: "Don't worry, Mom. We all have to die sometime." Of course our daughter was fine, and we have laughed about his calm assurances ever since.

If you make your family a priority in your life, you can never tell when one of those special memories will occur. Enjoy every minute of your children's lives, and they will bless your life. By the way, spending time with your children is a major key in their moral development. The more quality time you spend with them, the more they will accept your moral values, and the more they will love you. When we talk about quality time, it is important to remember that we will never find those quality moments if we don't spend a large *quantity* of time with them. Remember, your children will only be young once.

Rejoice in the beauty of God's creation. Regrettably we live in a world that is traveling a hundred miles an hour. If we lost our daytime planner, the world would collapse on us. As one young man explained, he went to work before his kids got out of bed and returned about thirty minutes before their bedtime. There are just not enough hours in the day.

Many of us get up by 5:30 or 6:00 a.m. to get some badly needed exercise so we can rush to work. Work occupies us all day with only a few minutes for a business lunch. Then we rush to the ball game just in time to see a little of the kid's game, charge to the house for a late meal, and rush the kids through baths so they can get to bed. When they are finally tucked in, we are exhausted. In this exhausted state, we now have a minute to acknowledge our mate, whom we haven't seen all day. After a minute or two of talking, we collapse into bed for a little rest before we start again tomorrow.

Not a good way to live! Slow down! Enjoy life! Take the time to enjoy your family and look at the relaxing beauty of God's world.

> O Lord, our Lord, how majestic is your name in all the earth! You have set your glory above the heavens. From the lips of children and infants you have ordained praise because of your enemies, to silence the foe and the avenger. When I consider your heavens, the work of your fingers, the moon and the stars, which your have set in place, what is man that you are mindful of him, the son of man that you care for him? You have made him a little lower than the heavenly beings and crowned him with glory and honor (Ps. 8:1–5).

Why not take the time to enjoy life? You will be more efficient at work, and your family will love spending time with you!

Rejoice because He has given us the hope of eternity. Although the earth is beautiful, it is nothing to compare with the beauty of heaven! If you are a faithful Christian, look with joy at the promise God has given you of eternal life. How could Christians ever get discouraged or down when they are thinking about the victory in heaven? Listen to what Peter said about our future:

Praise be to the God and Father of our Lord Jesus Christ! In his great mercy he has given us new birth into a living hope through the resurrection of Jesus Christ from the dead, and into an inheritance that can *never perish, spoil or fade—kept in heaven for you*, who through faith are shielded by God's power until the coming of the salvation that is ready to be revealed in the last time" (1 Pet. 1:3–5; emphasis added).

Did you notice the words? It will never perish. Our inheritance in heaven is eternal, and nothing can ever destroy it. It never gets old or useless. When you buy a new car or a new house, it looks great, but look at it in a few years. The car doesn't run right, and the house needs new paint and carpet. Not so with heaven! It is as beautiful five thousand years from now as it is today. It will never fade. Heaven, according to John in Revelation, is illuminated by the glory of God. (See Rev. 21:23.) That light will never go out.

Think about it, Christ Himself keeps your home in heaven prepared for you. (See Jn. 14:1–3.) About 11:00 p.m. one night, I stopped at a motel in Tennessee, expecting my room to be ready. What a surprise! They had no record of my reservation. I was tired and unhappy when they directed me to the next town some forty miles away. When you step up to the gates of heaven, that's not going to happen. Your home has been kept ready just for you. If you belong to God, rejoice in your living hope of eternity!

SUMMARY

As individual Christians, we can restore the concept of true fidelity in our homes. When we discuss fidelity in marriage, we are talking about more than just sexual faithfulness. It includes building relationships that are built on all the positive characteristics of love described in I Corinthians 13.

In order for families to become strong again, each family must find a real sense of purpose. Each family has a reason for existence. Each family should outline a way in which it will uniquely impact the world for good. Finding that purpose and uniting a family in a worthwhile cause will strengthen the family unit. Each family needs to take the time to write a family mission statement. How will this family bless our community, our church, and our world?

For families to flourish in today's society, they must also relearn the simple pleasure of having fun together. People are constantly bombarded with negatives. We hear about natural disasters, terrorist attacks, and corruption all the time. Family should be a safe haven away from the world's problems. Families should enjoy loving and caring for each other without the stress of the world destroying their peace of mind. Enjoy the love of your mate; enjoy the lives of your children; enjoy the beauty of God's creation; and enjoy the hope of eternal life, which God gives us.

STUDY GUIDE: CHAPTER 5
REBUILDING THE FAMILY
OF THE AMERICAN DREAM

I. Discuss the following passages:
  A. I Corinthians 13:1–8
    1. Why is patience important in a relationship?
    2. What acts of kindness do you consider important in your relationship?
    3. Which of the characteristics of love do you consider the most important? Why?
    4. How do you demonstrate that characteristic to your mate?
    5. With all of the divorces today, how do you explain Paul's statement that love never fails?
  B. Ephesians 5:22–33
    1. Explain what it means to submit to another person.
    2. In our society today, should wives still submit to their husbands? Why? Why not?
    3. Describe the love of Christ for His church.
    4. How can you tell if a man loves his wife the way Christ loves the church?

II. How important are faithfulness and purity in marriage?
   A. What does a person gain by being faithful to one person for his or her entire life?
   B. Why is it important for young people to be pure when they get married?
   C. What effect does an affair have on a marriage?
   D. What do you consider the greatest joy of having a good marriage and a loving family?

III. Spend the remaining time in class discussing ways you can strengthen families in your church.
   A. What can be done to help families spend more time together?
   B. What can be done to help families communicate better?
   C. What can be done to help families enjoy their lives more?
   D. What can be done to improve intimacy in marriages?
   E. What classes can you start in your congregation to help improve families?

IV. Personal plan of action
   A. Read I Corinthians 13 out loud to your family members, inserting your name as the one who will love them and their names as the ones to be loved. Make sure that they know that you are promising to love them in the manner described.
   B. Look at the factors that we have discussed which strengthen marriage, and consider if they are present in your home.
   C. Write down five things you are going to do in the next year to make your home a place filled with happiness.
   D. Write down five things you appreciate about each member of your family. Tell him or her why these things make him or her special.

STEP THREE: IGNITING MORAL COURAGE

6
The Collapse of our Moral Strength

> "It is curious that physical courage should be so common in the world and moral courage so rare."
> —Mark Twain

He stormed into my office and paced back and forth without saying a word. I looked at him and asked, "Can I help you?" He just kept pacing for another couple of minutes before he announced, "I need to smoke a cigarette." With that statement, he headed out the door. When I asked the secretary who the man was, she responded by saying she had never seen him before. In a few minutes, he was back in my office, standing, then sitting, then standing again. He finally announced that his name was Roger and he was an alcoholic. His situation was desperate. He had been picked up three times for driving while intoxicated, so he was spending every weekend in jail, with the court allowing him to work during the week in an effort to save his business. Because of his drinking problem, he owed a small fortune to creditors, not to mention fifty thousand dollars in back taxes.

The drinking and the financial problems were only the beginning of his challenges. Roger's six-year-old son, whom he adored, was being taken away from him. He quickly admitted that as an alcoholic who was still drinking regularly, he had no right to custody of the boy. His wife had already moved in with another man, and Roger realized that his son would be raised in a terrible environment if he didn't do something. He had to make a radical change in his life, and he knew it.

I wondered, "What in the world am I going to tell this guy? How can anyone get out of a mess like this?" Sure enough, he asked The Question: "What can I do to change the direction of my life completely?" "My answer was honest: "I don't know." However, I also told him that the apostle Paul had written an extremely interesting little letter to explain to people how they could change their thinking and have peace of mind by focusing on God. Roger and I spent the next three months studying the four short chapters in the Book of Philippians.

The change in Roger was remarkable. He started attending Alcoholics Anonymous, began to apply himself to his business, and started praying regularly for his son. The most challenging event during Roger's transformation came about two months into our study. He came in one morning and announced that his wife and her new love were taking his son and moving to California. He was devastated. This was the natural time to give up and start drinking again. However, instead of drinking, Roger continued to pray with great determination and faith. In his heart, he knew God had the power to bring his son back home. He was totally committed to building a life for himself and his son.

Another challenge arose while his son was in California. Roger was encouraged by his financial advisers to file for bankruptcy rather than pay off his huge debts. When we discussed honesty and integrity, he agreed that a Christian would always honor his responsibilities, so he set out on a long-term plan to pay off every debt, including his back taxes.

The evidence of God working in his life was plain to see: Roger increased his faith, became active in church, and started paying off his debt. His ex-wife got tired of having a little boy tagging along and sent him back to his father. Today, twenty years later, Roger hasn't had another drink; he is a respected businessman with a son who is a fine Christian. He is a man of great moral courage. He knew what he had to do, and he had enough courage to do it!

Remember the ripple effect that we want to start? The effect of this one man's life is remarkable. Roger has helped another man overcome his problem with alcohol and become a Christian, who in turn converted his wife to Christ. Roger also was involved in helping Nancy, a single mother with two boys, one of whom is seriously mentally challenged. Largely because of

Roger's influence, Nancy is a Christian and a member of a congregation that surrounds her and her sons with love, support, and encouragement. It's amazing, the impact that one person with moral courage can have!

While all of us would like to have the courage to live up to this principle, moral courage can be difficult to possess. We cannot stop the tidal wave of negative values unless we have the courage to act on our beliefs. Mark Twain once said, "It is curious that physical courage should be so common in the world and moral courage so rare." There are several reasons why moral courage is so rare.

THE FEAR OF BEING NARROW-MINDED

Those who choose to live a lifestyle that will lower the morals of our country are continuously pointing a finger at Christians and accusing us of being narrow-minded. Before we accept that label, we might want to take a closer look at narrow-mindedness. Those who are narrow-minded are the ones who are always throwing rocks at other people and bashing their way of life. But who's throwing rocks at whom?

It appears that, in our society, homosexuals and other groups who consistently talk about those terrible, judgmental Christians are hurling many of the rocks at Christians. Who is judging whom? I am aware that many times Christian people have acted in non-Christian ways by being harsh, hateful, and judgmental. It seems that the "free thinkers" and the "harsh, narrow-minded conservatives" are just two sides of the same coin.

People who stand for Christian principles, however, are those people who stand on God's moral law with the same love and kindness that Jesus presented to the world. Remember, Jesus told us to love our enemies and pray for those who persecute us (Mt. 5:43, 44). Paul expounded on that by telling us to overcome evil with good (Rom. 12:21). The most loving thing a person can do is to help someone correct a life pattern that is destructive and harmful to his or her soul.

One morning, I received a telephone call from a good friend. She was totally in a panic, crying, "Bill [her husband] is leaving.

What can I do?" My reply was: "Leave the house. I'm coming over to talk with him." When I arrived, Bill was packing his bags and getting ready to leave his wife and three children. We sat down and talked for over an hour. He explained his reasons for leaving, while I explained what he could expect as a result of his actions. I talked with him about how wrong his actions were according to God's law. Then I discussed with him the effect that his actions would have on his children, including the fact they would possibly lose their faith in God and lose their souls in the process. We talked about his soul and the fact that he was separating himself from God.

After our conversation, he called his wife and asked for her forgiveness. Since that time he has had a good marriage and reared some fine children. Bill has thanked me many times for the serious talk we had that day. It was neither narrow-minded nor harsh to talk with this man about the mistake he was about make and the way it would destroy both him and his family.

CONFUSION OVER WHAT IS RIGHT

With all the double messages in our society, Christians are often afraid to stand up for their faith because they are confused about what is right. As I discussed in Chapter 2, there are hundreds of double messages floating into our lives. Even in the religious world, there are all types of new ideas and new beliefs. How can we ever know that we are on solid ground when we take a stand? There really is an answer!

We can know we are right when we allow God to direct our hearts. The writer of the Book of Hebrews states, "For the word of God is living and active. Sharper than any double-edged sword, it penetrates even to dividing soul and spirit, joints and marrow; it judges the thoughts and attitudes of the heart" (Heb. 4:12). Remember, life's problems are complex, but the solutions are simple. If we are willing to surrender our will to God's and follow His Word, we will always be on solid ground when we take action.

THE COLLAPSE OF OUR MORAL STRENGTH

FEAR OF THE GHOSTS OF THE PAST

When a person stands up against immorality, he or she can be sure that those on the other side of the coin will look for any possible way to discredit him or her. Those who have no standards will have no problem attacking Christians who may have made mistakes in the past. This can affect relationships with family; it can be embarrassing and add terrible stress to life.

As he prepared for his second term as president, George W. Bush tried to appoint Bernard Kerik to a cabinet post. Immediately, Mr. Kerik's whole life became an open book, and the ghosts of the past killed the nomination and became an embarrassment to Mr. Kerik and to the President. Honestly, this may be one of the major reasons why so many good moral people are afraid to stand up and be counted. Being haunted by the past may destroy a person's future.

This type of fear is not a problem for the person who has absolutely nothing to be ashamed of in his past. However, almost everyone has made some serious mistakes, so how do we overcome our fear of the skeletons in the closet?

First, we must look at the future for our children and realize that their future depends on the moral direction of our country. Their future is worth the risk of someone discovering wrongs in our past. The moral decline of our nation is fueled by the fears of good people who are hiding what has happened in the past. If you decide that the future of your children is worth the risk, how can you be sure that the discovery of secrets in your past will not destroy your family? The answer rests comfortably in the awesome power of God. If you will take the time to explain to your children how harmful those past mistakes have been, it becomes a great lesson for them as you make clear the importance of every decision made in life.

You see, the whole issue is a matter of faith: Do we really trust God with our lives? The Proverbs writer exhorted, "Trust in the Lord with all your heart and lean not on your own understanding; in all your ways acknowledge him, and he will make your path straight" (Prov. 3:5, 6). The solution to our dilemma is to turn our future over to God by doing what is right and trusting Him with the outcome. When people have great faith, God is able to do great things in their lives.

Remember our God is a God of second chances. Look carefully at the lives of the heroes of the Bible, and you find over and over that they made mistakes. Abraham, Jacob, David, Paul, Peter—all had sinned in the past, and the list could go on and on. God uses people who have turned to him regardless of past sins. He will not only forgive you of your past, He will protect your future. Trust Him!

FEAR OF INCOMPETENCE

We all know ourselves pretty well; therefore, we have a reason to fear our lack of ability. We feel that we are not as capable as other people, so we wonder how we could take the lead in building the moral fabric of our country. What if we make mistakes, what if our weaknesses become apparent to other people? Are we going to fail because we are not as intelligent or as charismatic or as organized as someone else? The point is not your capabilities; the point is the value of the goal you plan to accomplish. The goal—the way it changes the lives of people you love—is all that matters. The key is to forget yourself and look at the importance of the goal.

My wife and I had just moved to a new location where I was going to preach for a church, which, although not large by most standards, was much larger than the one where I had been preaching. My mother-in-law came to visit, and we took her on a tour of the church building. As we walked though the auditorium, she looked at the balcony and remarked, "Man, this is a big place; you'd better not make any mistakes. Aren't you afraid?" (Mothers-in-law have a special way of humbling their sons-in-law!) "Of course I will make mistakes; I always do," was my response; then I added, "But it doesn't matter! If the people who come here are touched by the message of Christ, my mistakes and weaknesses won't matter. The only thing that matters is the cause of Christ."

When we focus too much on ourselves, our lack of ability disturbs us and causes us to veer away from the goal. Don't worry about what you can or cannot do: Look at the task! Focus on the goal! Accomplishing a worthy goal is all that matters. God will provide the proper outcome in His time.

SUMMARY

Fear is the worst of all motivations. Four great fears are destroying the ability of our people to act with integrity. These powerful fears include the fear of being considered narrow-minded, the fear that we don't really understand what is right, the fear that our past mistakes will be exposed, and the fear that we are not competent enough to make a strong stand for what we believe. The answer to all these fears is found in God. Our God is an awesome, almighty God, who is capable of relieving all of these fears. There are many motivations for our actions, the worst of those motivations being fear. Fear destroys peace of mind; it paralyzes our ability to accomplish good and causes us to accept evil without a fight.

STUDY GUIDE: CHAPTER 6
THE COLLAPSE OF OUR MORAL STRENGTH

I. Discuss the following passages:
   A. Matthew 26:69–75
      1. Why do you think Peter denied Christ?
      2. Why would he be afraid?
      3. How did he respond when he realized what he had done?
      4. What emotions do you see in Peter during the arrest, trial, and crucifixion of Jesus? Courage? Fear? Remorse? Shame? Sadness?
   B. Acts 4:8–22 and 5:25–42
      1. What changed Peter?
      2. What emotions do you think Peter had when he stood up for Christ?
      3. Do you think most Christians today act like the Peter

who denied Christ or like the Peter who bravely preached about Him? Why?
4. Which Peter do you resemble? The one who fearfully denied Christ, or the one who bravely proclaimed his message?

II. In your opinion, why do Americans lack moral courage?
   A. Which of the four reasons given in this chapter do you think has the most impact on people?
   B. What other factors cause people to be unwilling to stand up for what they believe?
   C. How does a person's past affect his ability to stand up for what he believes is right?

III. What are ways we can develop moral courage?
   A. What are the purposes that drive your life? Why are they important to you?
   B. How can you set an example of moral courage for the people you love?
   C. Which area do you think needs the most attention in your community?
      1. Setting better examples for our children?
      2. Improving morals in our schools?
      3. Helping the local government to develop a moral conscience?
      4. Stopping discrimination against Christians?
      5. Sharing our Christian faith?

IV. Personal plan of action:
   A. Make a list of your greatest fears.
   B. Take that list of fears to God in prayer every night for one week.
   C. Start reading the great victory passages in the Bible.
   D. Talk with your family about your fears and your plans to accomplish something great for the Lord.
   E. Once you have prayed every evening for a week about your fears, wad up your list and deposit it where it belongs—in the trash!

7
Inspiring Americans to Live With Moral Courage

"When we refuse to confront today, we create a bigger problem for tomorrow. Whenever we back away from a problem, it doesn't go away or get better—it festers and gains power."—Robert E. Staub

The people of our nation need only a little inspiration to become strong people with great integrity. In this chapter, we will examine three practical keys to igniting moral courage in our friends and family.

In one congregation where I preached, we had an absolutely fantastic children's Bible Hour. The director of the program, Daniel, was a young man who was intelligent, energetic, imaginative, and had a terrific way with children. The kids loved his exciting puppet shows and his great teaching, and, more importantly, they learned to love God. Daniel, however, was not a great detail person. He could develop the ideas and do the teaching, but putting together the stage, making sure the costumes were ready, and getting the equipment lined up was just not his thing.

That's when one of the greatest Christians I have ever met entered the picture. Steve didn't have the same imagination or skill with the children that Daniel possessed, but he had a great love for the children and a devotion to God. Steve was the silent power behind the great teaching program. He was always present, always willing do anything that was needed, running back and forth to the store, picking up needed items, staying up late to run off scripts for the next drama, or making sure the stage was set up and ready. Whatever was needed, Steve was the go-to man!

Although everyone gave Daniel credit for building a great Bible Hour program, the real backbone of the program was Steve and others who humbly worked toward the goal of giving our children an opportunity to know God. Steve's impact on the future of hundreds of children has been tremendous. Don't be afraid of your weaknesses; look at the goal and go to work! Not everyone can be the front man, and not everyone needs to be! God is powerful enough to use the abilities we have without worrying about the abilities we don't have!

As we overcome our fears, there are three avenues available to help us develop true courage. If we examine each of these areas, I believe they will bring out a passion in us, enabling us to forget our fears and take action to accomplish the rebuilding of the moral strength of our nation. Remember—desire is more important than ability, and attitude is more important than facts. Average people who take action for godly goals do great things.

Remember Andrew in the Bible? We have no recorded sermons that he preached. He was not in the Lord's inner circle, and he is only mentioned a few times in the Bible. However, Andrew was the one who brought Peter to the Lord! Without Andrew, Peter would never have spoken on the day of Pentecost, and those three thousand people who had all their sins washed away by being baptized into Christ would never have been born again. Never look at your weakness. Always focus your attention on God. If you step out in faith, God will supply all you need to accomplish His goals!

THREE ESSENTIALS FOR MORAL COURAGE

1. A Willingness to Take Risks for a Worthwhile Purpose

To define moral courage, there must be a purpose greater than ourselves, we must set an example of courage for those we love, and we must take action in the areas of our lives that will affect the future. If we are concerned with losing our positions in society or our wealth, we will crumble. Robert E. Staub states:

> The real question is "When it comes down to it, will you have the courage to act, to put yourself on the line?" The courage to act is the willingness to place yourself in harm's way and this requires the willingness to leave the safety of being a spectator and to enter the arena. It

requires the courage to commit yourself and your heart, and to enter a profound relationship with life.[1]

We will find that type of courage only if we look beyond ourselves and see something worthy of risk. The men and women of the "Greatest Generation" believed that democracy and freedom were worth whatever it cost, even their lives. I believe that re-energizing the moral conscience of our society is worth the risk of facing opposition in courts, in public debate, or in any area of our lives. What do you think? Is it worth your best efforts to help your children and grandchildren live in a country that encourages Christian moral standards, or should we just give up?

Paul defiantly refused when I told him to sit down and listen. He was only ten years old, but his look of hatred and anger was that of a hardened criminal. He had come to our latchkey program from his present foster home. It was the twenty-third such placement for him. He was an expert at lying, stealing, cheating, and disrupting class. By the time he had been with us for two weeks, it was obvious that Paul's problems were far too serious for our volunteers to handle, and we had to ask him to leave our program. My heart aches for Paul and other damaged children; it's distressing to see a ten-year-old child who is already becoming a criminal. We can do better! We can't save all the children like Paul, but we can save some. Are you willing to help?

Although I am still heartsick over Paul, I also remember little Tonya. Twelve-year-old Tonya arrived kicking and screaming, wearing a very short miniskirt and a blouse that had a picture of a painted-up rock group on the front. She yelled out her hatred of our church and all the workers who were involved in our program. She physically fought with her mother as she was forced to sign up for after-school care. "I hate you" seemed to be her favorite expression. When she told Doris McGill how much she hated her, Doris responded, "I know you do, honey, but I love you."

---

[1]Robert E. Staub, *The Seven Acts of Courage: Bold Leadership for a Wholehearted Life* (Provo, Utah: Executive Excellence, 1999), 139.

When Tonya was in high school, we all laughed about that first day. She was now a beautiful Christian girl volunteering her time to help other children who needed to be loved. Because of the change in Tonya's life, her mother had become a Christian, her brother had become a Christian, and her father, an alcoholic, had stopped drinking. Believe me, one Tonya is worth all the disappointments of the Pauls in the world. Will you make a difference in someone's life?

2. The Willingness to Set an Example of Courage For Those We Love

A second essential is that we must work on becoming the type of person who will motivate those we love to live with courage. Because most of us will stand and defend the people we love, moral courage is all about loving people. Jesus was sent to the earth because "God so loved the world" (Jn. 3:16a).

Little Megan took hold of my hand and said, "Dean, play basketball with me." She was four years old at the time and had one of those basketball goals that stood about three feet high. She was smiling from ear to ear, and I couldn't resist the opportunity to put other things aside and play basketball.

She went to the basket, dribbled the ball off her foot, and ran after it. Retrieving the ball, she returned with the same smile and enthusiasm, only to bounce the ball off her foot again. Once again she retrieved the ball and ran back with the same excitement, but this time she raised the ball over her head and tried to throw it. I caught the ball and dropped it into the basket.

When Megan saw the ball go through the hoop, she ran to her mother, yelling, "Mommy, Mommy, I made a basket!" She is a smiling, happy little girl being reared by godly parents. Do you think little children who are abused or in broken homes or are left without loving guidance will have that same joy in their lives?

The next generation deserves the chance to grow up with the light of joy still shining in its eyes. It will not happen if children are reared without loving parents. It will not happen if they are abused by pedophiles. It will not happen if they live in an environment filled with drugs, drunkenness, and immorality.

We must have the courage to help build happy homes for the Megans of the next generation. Look at your children, and ask yourself, "What type of nation do I want them to inherit from my generation?" Then look even deeper, and ask yourself, "What influences do I want affecting their eternal souls?" The answer to that question should give you the courage to take action.

When we have looked beyond ourselves to examine God's purpose in our lives, and have been motivated by the well-being of the people we love, then we must begin to take courageous action in the areas of life which will impact their world and their spiritual lives.

3. A Willingness to Take Action in Areas That Affect the Future

We need to look hard at the people we love the most and ask ourselves whether or not we love them enough to impact their future.

Do you love your family enough to take action to impact their future?

There are five areas in which we must demonstrate courage if we are going to impact the future of the people we love:

1. We must have the courage to be the moral patterns for our children.
2. We must have the courage to reclaim our schools.
3. We must have the courage to redirect our government.
4. We must have the courage to stop the reverse discrimination that is aimed at Christians today.
5. We must share our faith with others.

The first area in which we must develop courage is in our own homes. As we have already discussed in an earlier chapter, you must have the courage to be the role model for your children. In his book *The Moral Intelligence of Children*, Pulitzer Prize-winning author, Robert Coles, states,

> The most persuasive moral teaching we adults do is by example; the witness of our lives, our ways of being with others and speaking to them and getting on with them—all of that is taken in slowly, cumulatively, by our sons and daughters, our students.[2]

He continues, "In the long run of a child's life, the unselfconscious moments that are what we think of simply as the unfolding events of the day and the week turn out to be the really powerful and persuasive times, morally."[3] If we don't have the courage on a daily basis to live truth in our own lives, we will never see good moral behavior in our children's lives. If you need verification of this, just take a few minutes to observe television commercials, programs, and movies, and see the way kids are presented. They rule! They are presented as arrogant, disrespectful, sloppy, vulgar-mouthed people who have the right to do and say whatever they want.

As parents, we must have the courage to lead our children toward the moral standards of God. Today many parents are trying hard to be their children's best friends rather than parents. To be a parent, we lovingly lead our children in a direction of moral maturity and decisively correct them when they select a path that will harm them.

Remember, self-esteem is not built by allowing children to do as they please; it is built by helping them live up to the standards that God has set for us. When they live up to those standards, they will have a great feeling of confidence and security. Paul told his beloved Timothy, "The goal of this command is love, which comes from a pure heart and a good conscience and a sincere faith" (1 Tim. 1:5).

It is only when children grow up with a pure heart that they are able to enjoy life and make their parents proud. Paul also stated that Timothy had faith in God because he had learned it from his family: "I have been reminded of your sincere faith,

---

[2] Robert Coles, *The Moral Intelligence of Children* (New York: Random House, 1997), 31.
[3] Ibid.

which first lived in your grandmother Lois and in your mother Eunice and, I am persuaded, now lives in you also" (2 Tim. 1:5). Parents must have the courage to live in a way that leads their children to develop pure hearts and a good conscience. As parents, we must develop the courage to confront.

Robert Staub expresses this thought:

> When we refuse to confront today, we create a bigger problem for tomorrow. Whenever we back away from a problem, it doesn't go away or get better—it festers and gains power. It destroys our power to act. When we avoid painful situations, we inflict damage on our souls and compromise our integrity.[4]

Not only do we damage our souls by refusing to deal with critical issues, we terminally damage the ability of our children to face their problems with courage. Parents, stand up for what is right! Lead your children toward a life of moral courage and integrity.

Good, moral people must have the courage to reclaim our schools. In most American towns and cities, over 90 percent of our people believe in God, so why can't we say the Lord's Prayer in a public setting? With 90 percent of our people believing in God, why can't a teacher talk about the Ten Commandments or the biblical account of creation? This is a democracy, and in a democracy the majority of the people have the right to be heard. It is time to stop allowing the minority to run our schools.

Before we go too far in this area, however, we need to address the concerns that have caused the Bible and Christianity to be kicked out of our schools. First, there is a concern that teachers or students will force their religion on other people. The whole idea of separation of church and state is not to keep faith in God out of our government or our schools; it is to keep one person from forcing his religion on another person. With careful observation, it is easy to make sure that no one takes advantage of the situation to force his or her views on others.

---

[4]Staub, 67.

The second concern is that those who do not believe in God will be discriminated against or otherwise mistreated. Christianity is a religion where love overcomes evil; therefore, it will not cause more problems when God is openly discussed in our schools; it will cause less discrimination and more interaction as students of other beliefs are allowed to share their ideas. When this happens, there will be *fewer* problems, not more. If we are to reclaim our schools, we must be careful to guard against developing a society that is harmful to those who have other beliefs.

With that in mind, we should never doubt the fact that all teachers impact the lives and moral values of their students. You can be sure that if Johnny's favorite teacher is a homosexual, Johnny will know it, and his view of homosexuality will change radically. If we are to protect our children, we must insist on the right of a school board and the school administration to ask personal questions of prospective teachers. As a preacher, I once read, "Preaching is presenting truth through personality." Look at good teachers, and you will see that their personalities impact their teaching. The kids learn because they respond to the person, which means they will also pick up the worldview and attitudes of that teacher.

The curriculum will also have an effect on the moral lives of our children. A few years ago, the school my children attended decided to show Magic Johnson's film on sex education to all the students. Before showing the film, they were kind enough to allow parents to view the film and make suggestions. Very few parents attended, but the ones who were present got an eye full. I'm not sure how to define pornography legally, but I was totally embarrassed to be viewing such a filthy presentation. With rap songs and dancing condoms, every aspect of sex was presented in an irreverent and mocking manner.

Is this the way we are going to explain sexual relationships to our children? When the other parents and I saw the film, we were convinced that there must be a better way to teach our children about the proper relationship between sex, love, and life. Working together with the school administration, we were able to form a committee of teachers and parents that reviewed different approaches to sex education. As a result, the school adopted an abstinence-based sex education program which was much more appropriate for our young people and much more in line with the moral attitudes of our community.

Over the years, I have discovered that most of our school administrators and teachers share our concerns about the proper way to educate our children and produce good citizens. When parents attack schools for what they are teaching, the school administrators will react just as you and I would—by defending their actions. On the other hand, when concerned parents say to educators, "We have concerns and want to work with you to produce the best possible education for our children," the result is usually a community effort which produces a good school environment.

The political and social realm of our society also demands our bold and aggressive action. If we truly care about the future of our children, we must be motivated to stand up in our political and social arenas. The things happening in our communities will affect the future of our children. On a city and county level, it is people like us who will elect the leaders, and we have the right and the responsibility to make sure they are men and women of good character. We must have the courage to stand for our belief in God. Our nation was founded—and has become strong—based on the courage of people who had great faith in our Creator. God is an integral part of our heritage, and without His blessings, our nation would not exist. In his inaugural address, George Washington demonstrated his dependence on God when he stated,

> It would be peculiarly improper to omit in this first official act my fervent supplications to the Almighty Being who rules over the Universe, who presides in the Council of Nations, and whose providential aids can supply every human defect, that His benediction may consecrate the liberties and happiness of the people of the United States, a government instituted by themselves.[5]

---

[5]Quoted in D. P. Diffine, "One Nation Under God," *The Entrepreneur*, A quarterly journal for the Belden Center for Private Enterprise Education, Harding University, Searcy, Ark. (February 2006) 4.

Benjamin Franklin added strength to our country's commitment to God when he said, "Here is my creed. I believe in one God, the Creator of the Universe. That he governs it by His providence. That he ought to be worshipped."[6] In 1802, Thomas Jefferson provided this warning for the good of our nation: "Can the liberties of a nation be secure when we have removed a conviction that these liberties are a gift of God?"[7] It is essential for good, moral, God-loving people to stand up in the political realm and mold the laws and leadership of this country. I am not advocating a violation of separation of church and state. The requirements of separation were not established to keep religion out of government; they were established to prevent the government from forcing one religion on people to the exclusion of other religions.

A wise politician once explained that it only takes 2 percent of the population to win an election. If there are 2 percent of the people who are highly vocal and totally committed to an issue, they will influence enough people to win an election. In the past two decades, a minority of people in our country, because they are continuously demanding rights, has forced upon the American people a number of laws that are opposed to our basic values. It is encouraging to see the recent trend of good, moral people beginning to speak up, taking a stand for moral principles.

The stand begins with *you* in the smallest political setting possible. You have influence in your community and your county, so that is the place to start. Local and county officials are the quickest to respond to the actions of people. When you and ten other people stand up for something on a local or county level, it has a great impact. If you are opposed to abortion, elect county judges and other officials who are opposed to abortion! If you are opposed to same-sex marriages, elect county judges and local officials who are opposed to same sex-marriage (and who are not afraid to state that belief)! If no one is running who holds your views, get a few friends together and find someone to run.

---

[6]Ibid., 14.
[7]Ibid., 17.

When enough cities and counties stand up for moral values, the national politicians will begin to recognize the trends. Always remember that politicians want to be elected, and when they see a trend developing, they will quickly jump on the bandwagon.

We must be bold enough to stop reverse discrimination against Christians. In many arenas today, every view is acceptable except that of those who believe in Christ. Christians are free game for anyone who wants to slander those "narrow-minded, bigoted Bible bangers." Why do Christians put up with such talk? Why don't we take a stand and demand the same respect that others receive in our politically correct society?

A fifth area in which we must develop courage is the willingness to share our faith. It seems that more and more Christian people have begun to hide their faith. It is unpopular to talk about Christ in our society; after all, if you are sharing Christ, you must believe something else is wrong. In a society that treasures tolerance, we have been convinced that we must not try to persuade others that Christianity is the best lifestyle. The truth is, if we really love people, we will try to share with them the very best way to have true, lasting happiness.

Over the years, I have been beside many people who were coming to the end of their lives on this earth. Some of them had lived without Christ, and they were filled with regret and fear. They had regrets over the relationships they had destroyed, the people who had been hurt, and the lives that had been harmed by their actions. They were no longer interested in their wealth or accomplishments; they just looked back, wishing they could try again. As they look forward to eternity, there is only fear. Without a faith in God, what happens after death? They have no hope and no assurance, and as far as they are concerned, everything is over, and they have failed.

I have also been at the bedside of many Christians who were preparing to die, and the scene is entirely different. At about 7 p.m. on a Monday, I received a call from Irene Rose, who said, "Dean, I want you to come see me." Although Irene was seriously ill in the hospital, there was no panic or fear in her voice, so I responded, "Irene, I plan on coming to the hospital tomorrow." She insisted, however, that I needed to come that night. Although there was no real stress in her voice, I could tell she really wanted to talk to me as soon as possible, so I headed for the hospital.

When I arrived, Irene was smiling. After a short period of friendly small talk, she thanked me for coming and explained that she was going to die before the next morning. She wanted to let all her family and friends know how much she loved them and how happy she was to be going home to heaven. There was total peace in her eyes as she spoke. God had blessed her life; she had won the victory, and it was the right time for her to go home. She died peacefully later that night, without regrets and without fear. The Christian life is the best life; we should care enough about other people to share our faith!

My wife's grandfather, Enoch Ware, was one of my favorite people. He was the only man I have ever known who started preaching at the age of eighty. I met him when he was eighty-two, and for the few remaining years of his life, he shared with me the joys of belonging to God. He loved to talk about his children and grandchildren, so I learned about their families and their faith. He was especially proud of the fact that up until the time of his death, there had never been a divorce in the family. As he approached death, there was no regret, no fear—only victory. The Christian life is the best life; we should care enough about people to share our faith!

Morris Misso was a retired builder who developed a rare form of leukemia and passed away a few months later. Although I knew Morris was a good man, I was totally amazed at the response to his death. When it appeared in the paper that I was to preach his funeral, calls started coming in from people all over Texas who had been helped by Morris. Some talked about how Morris had paid for their college education; others told about personal loans Morris had given them in times of special stress; some talked about the bicycles he bought every Christmas for the poor children in town. Morris won the victory, and he died without regret and without fear as he went home to the Lord. So I will repeat, the Christian life is the best way to live; do you care enough about people to share your faith?

We will also develop courage when we look not just into the future of our children and our country, but when we look into eternity. The purpose that drives us to look into the future should go even further than the next generation; it should carry us to a view of eternity. If you are convinced that your actions will change eternity for the people you work with and love, you will have the courage to take great risks and accept great challenges.

My son Keith is not the type who wants to go far away from home. He loves being with his family; he enjoys the holidays, family meals, family traditions, and everything that is associated with home. He does not like learning other languages, eating strange food, or living in different environments. That means he is *not* the type of person who usually leaves the comforts of home and heads to a mission field.

However, Keith and his wife, Michele, became convinced that they could serve the Lord by becoming a part of a mission team headed for Santiago, Chile. Fighting back the fears and concerns of leaving home, in March 1999, they flew from the DFW airport to Santiago, Chile, to help start a church.

Two of the first people they studied with and converted were Julio and Sylva Sandoval. This was a wonderful middle-aged couple that previously had no relationship with Christ. They quickly became leaders in the newly-formed congregation. It was then that the doctors discovered Sylva had a very aggressive type of cancer. Less than a year after the diagnosis, Sylva was with our Lord in heaven, and the church family was surrounding Julio with love and support. Think of that picture! Without the commitment of the mission team who went to Santiago, Sylva would have died without the hope of heaven; her husband would have been left to grieve without the hope of ever seeing her again. He wouldn't have had the love and support of his church family.

Keith and Michele and their mission team had impacted eternity. What if Keith had given in to his fears and concerns? What if Michele had refused to move to a different culture? What about you? Will your actions make any difference for eternity, or will you give in to your fears?

DEVELOPING A PLAN OF COURAGEOUS ACTION

All of this talk about courage and the areas in which we need to have courage will never translate into anything worthwhile unless we establish a plan of action. Courage is strengthened when there is a plan for reaching worthwhile objectives. Former US Army Ranger and Green Beret, Don Greene, in his book *Fight Your Fear and Win*, explains how training carefully and understanding your mission helps you to overcome fears. In the military, training is repeated over and over until each man knows exactly what he must do in every situation. When the enemy attacks, it is natural to be afraid; however, knowing the mission and knowing the proper response overrides the fear and allows the soldiers to react with courage.

As Greene explains, the Rangers' formula for action, which is referred to as the Four-Point Field Order, is this:

1. Assess the situation.
2. Determine the mission.
3. Figure out the execution and logistics.
4. Prepare for contingencies.[8]

When facing a difficult mission, the Four-Point Field Order guides the US Army Rangers. In the same way, our fears are conquered when we map out our plan of action to rebuild the moral backbone of our nation. On the following pages, a plan of action is presented to help you overcome your fears and take courageous action to help our country regain its moral compass.

1. List Specific Goals

The first step in courageous action is to write down the ultimate goals that you plan to accomplish. You will notice that I didn't say, "Write down the goals you hope to accomplish," or

---

[8]Don Greene, *Fight Your Fear and Win* (New York: Broadway Books, 2001), 24–25.

"Write down the goals you wish to accomplish." Courage is for those who will not accept defeat or failure. We are not thinking that maybe, possibly, or if we are lucky, these things can be done. We know that if these goals are within the *will* of God, they will be accomplished.

Never make any provisions for failure; negative thinking will destroy your resolve. When you write the ending first, you will have the courage to live toward that ending. That's right; first write down your ultimate goals. I believe everyone should take the time to write down the final analysis of his or her life. When it is all over, what have you accomplished? What will they say at your funeral? After you have written the final result of your life, start working on the specific accomplishments that will lead to that goal. Try writing your own obituary! What do you plan to leave as a legacy of your life?

As we work through this activity, you will want to follow the pattern on the following pages and fill in the blank chart. In three areas of your life, what do you plan to accomplish? First look at your *personal life*: What are you going to do that has an impact on eternity? Write down exactly what you plan to accomplish in your life. You remember we discussed the importance of a personal mission statement in an earlier chapter. If you are to accomplish anything, you must know where you are going. This is your destination; you have decided to buy your ticket, so write down where the ticket is taking you.

When you have written down that goal (or goals), look at your *family*. What are the most important objectives for each member of your family? Again, we must have an idea of where our family is going, or we will never be able to have the home we really desire. Write down the exact things you want for your family. Do you want your children to go to college? Do you want them to become Christians? Do you want them to have good marriages? What about your relationship with your mate? Do you want to have a warm, loving relationship? Do you want to travel? Do you want to retire and spend time together? Write out your most important goals for your family.

The third area of goal-setting is important because it has a positive or negative impact on the first two. Write down your goals for your *community*. Do you want schools that stand for moral values? Do you want a local government that cares about truth and justice? Do you want your community to have a positive impact on the moral development of our country? What is the biggest change that is needed in your community? If it is something you can affect, make that your goal.

2. Decide on Steps to Reach These Goals

The question is, Now that you have written the ending, how can you write the story that will cause that ending to occur? Goals are meaningless until specific steps are lined out to help us reach those goals. You want to break down each goal into five to ten steps that you must take in order to accomplish that specific goal. See the Sample Worksheet near the end of this chapter as an example of how to set up an order of activities that will allow you to accomplish each goal. Start with one simple, easy-to-accomplish step, and then move to the next step. A trip of a thousand miles starts with one step.

3. Set Up a Timetable to Accomplish Your Goals

We are great procrastinators! All of us set goals and then a year later wonder why we haven't accomplished them. The reason is we haven't set up a rigid timetable for our steps. We must have some guidelines that will lead us to complete our goals. Do you remember all of the time requirements in college? Tests were scheduled; papers were due on a certain date. There was no choice; you had to have the work done on those dates. People who accomplish important, meaningful objectives set timetables and expect to meet those requirements. There are two keys to setting up timetables. First, make sure that you have actually set aside enough time to accomplish the specific step you have been assigned. Second, be tough on yourself! Expect to accomplish the task in the assigned length of time, and don't make excuses.

4. Make a List of the People Who Will Help You Accomplish Your Goals

Any worthwhile goal will require the help of other good

people. If it is a family objective, your family will need to know what you are trying to accomplish. When they understand the importance of the goal, they will be ready and willing to accept the opportunity to help accomplish that goal for the good of your family. If your goal relates to the school or the community, again you will need strong support from people who know you and love you. Before any endeavor, *people* are the key to success! Average people working together for a great cause are powerful.

5. Contact the People Who Will Share Your Goals

You are not alone! Many Christian people who share your concerns would love to have an opportunity to help improve our communities and our country. They have just never been asked. Christian people are afraid to act because we often think we are standing alone. When you present your plan to other believers, not only will they be excited and willing to support the goals, they will make suggestions which will help you to refine your plan of action. Excitement and courage grow when a group of people work together for something great!

Dianna Welch, a wonderful Christian lady who was involved in a "dream class" which I was conducting, expressed her concern for the children who went home after school to an empty house. Studies have indicated that latchkey kids are at a greater risk of alcohol use, drug addiction, teenage pregnancies, and abuse. She wanted to do something but really didn't know how or where to start. Immediately, other people in the class began to share their concerns and ideas, and the result was the first church-sponsored latchkey program in the state of Texas. Over the past twenty years, hundreds of children have been blessed by the love and care of Christian people. Not only did our local congregation start taking care of latchkey kids, other churches started similar programs. There is no telling how many individuals have been inspired or helped because of Diana Welch's desire to help kids. Diana would never have been able to accomplish her dream if she hadn't gotten others involved.

6. Pray and Go to Work!

No dreams or worthwhile goals are ever accomplished without the blessings of God, so now is the time to discuss your plan with God. Since our God is in control of the universe, He is capable of helping you accomplish a meaningful goal. Remember what Paul said: "If God is for us, who can be against us?" (Rom. 8:31b), and, "In all these things we are more than conquerors through him who loved us" (Rom. 8:37). God works in us; He sends us out to accomplish His will, but you must start the project! Don't just talk about it! Go to work!

7. Write Down Your Method of Evaluation

How will you know that you have been successful? Some people set goals that cannot be evaluated, so they never really accomplish anything. For example, I know a man who said his personal goal was to be a better person, but when I asked him what that meant, he had no answer. If my goal is to be a better person, I must be able to identify how I can become better. I might evaluate my progress by stating that I have become a better person in the following ways:

1. I am spending two more hours a week with my family.
2. I will become a better parent in the following ways (list the specific ways).
3. I have spent fifteen minutes a day in Bible study and prayer.

If you have worked though your timeline and the goal is now complete, what new steps do you need to take to accomplish the goal? (Remember, you are not going to fail!) Now that you understand the pattern, look at the Sample Worksheet near the end of this chapter. After reading it, use the outline that follows the Sample Worksheet to start your own meaningful project. Be very specific as you work out each step. The objectives you accomplish could affect hundreds of lives!

SUMMARY

Developing moral courage is a difficult process. Americans sometimes lack moral courage for a number of reasons. As we have noted in the previous chapter, the first reason we lack it is our fear of negative consequences. When a person takes a stand on a moral issue, there will often be negative consequences. The value of being right with God and influencing our society for righteousness, however, will always outweigh the consequences. In order to maintain moral courage, a person must also be confident that he is doing the right thing. In a society that has difficulty understanding right and wrong, this can be very confusing. While others are accepting alternate lifestyles and ideas, people of moral courage must have a good grasp of truth in order to make the proper stand. If we are comfortable with our knowledge of the Bible and have a good understanding of God's Word, it will give us strength to stand on His principles. Even when one understands truth, there is the fear that when he stands for truth, those who oppose him will bring up inconsistencies from his past actions. These mistakes can be extremely embarrassing to someone with a reputation to uphold. Once again, however, we draw on the Lord for strength, realizing that when we do what is right, He will protect our future. The fourth reason we struggle to make a strong stand on moral issues is our fear that we are not competent to withstand the pressure from the other side. We often believe that someone else would be more capable of representing the truth than we would. Of course, when we give in to these feelings we are really slapping God in the face by denying Him the opportunity of working in our lives.

We have also outlined three important steps in developing moral courage. Moral courage begins with a simple but complete definition of our purpose in life. What important things does God plan for us to accomplish? When we have a well-defined path laid out for our lives, it will be possible for us follow that path as we use God's strength.

Once we have defined our specific purpose in life, we then turn our attention to setting the proper example for our children and our loved ones. Life is never a success if our children are not blessed by our personal strength. Regardless of all the other influences in their lives, our children's greatest influence is their parents. Our children gain the courage to live meaningful, productive lives when we model character and integrity through our own lifestyle.

As we set an example for our children, we must also be aware of the impact that the environment will have on our lives and the lives of our children. We cannot be people of moral courage if we do not get involved in improving our environment. People of moral courage will be involved in the important areas of life. Their activities will include working to improve schools, getting involved in local politics, and of course, being involved in the Lord's work at their local congregation. We have the power to make a difference in all these areas. However, our influence will be limited if we continue to allow others to discriminate against Christians. We must help the Christian community to get a fair voice in our society. Stopping the discrimination is not enough for people of true courage; we must also be willing to share with others our faith in God. Then our impact on eternity will be even greater than our impact in this life.

Our environment will never be changed unless we have a plan to impact each of the important areas of our lives. The plan should be carefully outlined with specific goals and a specific timeline for achieving those goals.

SAMPLE WORKSHEET TO ACCOMPLISH YOUR GOAL

Specific goal:

To develop a latchkey program that will provide safe, loving care for sixty elementary school-aged children every day after school.

Steps to accomplish the goal:

1. Get the approval of the church leaders to use the church outreach building.
2. Outline daily activities for the children.
3. Develop a discipline policy and rules for participation.
4. Select a director.
5. Get all necessary licenses and insurance.
6. Get volunteers.
7. Arrange for transportation.
8. Set up a budget and raise money.
9. Advertise the program to the community.
10. Sign up children.
11. Inform the parents of rules and regulations.

Timetable:

1. Steps 1 through 3 by June 3.
2. Steps 4 through 7 by June 21.
3. Steps 8 and 9 by July 21.
4. Steps 10 and 11 by August 9.
5. Start the program on the first day of school.

People who will help with the goal:

1. Mark and Dianna Welch
2. Joe and Trish Hayes
3. Jim and Carol Johnson

4. Seniors group in the church
   5. Teenagers from the church
   6. Sarah Smith
   7. Doris McGill

Date I will contact these people:

By June 1

My personal work time:

During the summer, I will spend every Monday morning from 8 a.m. until noon working through the steps of the plan. I will also reserve Tuesday evenings for meetings with workers. When school starts, I will assist the director two afternoons a week from 3:00 p.m. until 6:00 p.m.

Pray and go to work

I will pray for this program and call by name the volunteers and children at least once a week before I go to bed at night.

Evaluation:

We will be successful if we accomplish the following:

   1. Provide a safe environment for fifty to sixty elementary students after school.
   2. Help those students to improve their grades by an average of one letter grade.
   3. Help the children to improve their manners and behavior at home.
   4. Teach the children some basic principles of the Bible.
   5. Have at least one family start attending church services regularly.

A PLAN
FOR MY MOST IMPORTANT GOAL!

Specific goal:

Steps to accomplish the goal:

    1.
    2.
    3.
    4.
    5.
    6.

Timetable:

    1.
    2.
    3.
    4.
    5.

People who will help with the goal:

    1.
    2.
    3.
    4.
    5.

Date I will contact these people:

My personal work time:

Pray and go to work

Evaluation:

We will be successful if . . .

1.
2.
3.

STUDY GUIDE: CHAPTER 7
INSPIRING AMERICANS TO LIVE WITH MORAL COURAGE

I. Discuss the following passages:
   A. Job 1:13–22
      1. How did Job respond to his incredible disasters?
      2. How would a person who lacked faith respond in the same situation?
      3. How do you think you would respond?
      4. In what situations do you think it is the hardest to do what is right?
   B. I Samuel 17:41–51
      1. Why were the Israelites afraid of Goliath?
      2. Why was David's attitude different?
      3. Do you believe that God will fight for his people today as he fought for David? Why or why not?

II. Discuss the steps necessary to take action to improve the moral standards in your community.
   A. What are the seven steps necessary to accomplish an important goal?
   B. What are some possible goals for your class?
   C. Have the class discuss one or two important goals that you want to accomplish.

III. How will the accomplishment of your goal or goals affect eternity? Set up a timeline for accomplishing that goal.
   A. When will you start?
   B. When do you expect to finish?

IV. Take the remaining class time to work through a plan of action for the goal or goals you have set.

STEP FOUR:
RECLAIMING
OUR SCHOOLS

8
HOW COULD THIS HAPPEN IN OUR SCHOOLS?

The majority of our people have good moral values, and it's time for those people to restore discipline in our schools!

On March 21, 2005, high school teacher Diane Schwarz arrived at school expecting another average day of teaching. That same day, Ashley Morrison went to her classes, visiting with friends and taking part in the everyday life of a student. Before the day was over, both were lying on the floor behind the locked door of Ms. Schwarz's classroom, listening to the frightening sounds of a shotgun firing and an angry student trying to break down the door of the classroom.

Diane reported, "I got down on the floor and called the cops. I was still half in shock." At the same instant, Ashley had her cell phone out frantically calling her mother. "Mom, he's trying to get in here, and I'm scared." When the police arrived, a security guard, a teacher, and five students were dead and several others wounded. The shooter who also took his own life was Jeff Weise, who came to school after killing his grandfather and his grandfather's girlfriend. It was an unbelievable, horrible day at school. Since the Columbine High School shootings in April 1999, there have been thirty-four recorded school shootings, most of which have resulted in at least one death. How could this happen?

As educators have worked so hard to take fundamental religious values out of education, they have also taken away the moral character development of our young people. Schools have become dangerous places. My two children attended a high school where it was common knowledge that you never went into one of the restrooms. There was usually smoking, drugs, and an unsavory element hanging around in them. In fact, both of my children would drive home from school if they needed to use the restroom during school hours. That's a sad picture. It's time to reclaim our schools!

The backbone of our country is our school system. Our children will spend seven hours a day on 182 days a year for twelve years in school. During that time they will not only learn to read and write, but teachers, administrators, and other students will influence every aspect of their lives. The type of school they attend will affect their attitude about life.

When I was young, the local school was, to a large degree, a continuation of my home: The teacher believed in God; most of the other students came from intact homes; and the school administration was in touch with the feelings and concerns of the community. Regrettably, something has changed. Look at the chart below, which was adapted from Stephen Covey's excellent book, *The 7 Habits of Highly Effective Families,* and consider the changes that have taken place in our schools.[1]

Top Disciplinary Problems
According to Public School Teachers

1940	1990
Talking out of turn	Drug abuse
Chewing gum	Alcohol abuse
Making noise	Pregnancy
Running in the halls	Suicide
Cutting in line	Rape
Dress code infractions	Robbery
Littering	Assault

What happened? Why are we having such enormous problems in our schools? If we rewind the clock, we discover that a few intellectuals took the schools out of the hands of parents. When the scientific community tried to force belief in God out of schools during the debates on Darwin's theory of evolution,

---

[1] Stephen Covey, *The 7 Habits of Highly Effective Families* (New York: Golden Books, 1997), 17.

our whole education system changed. As William Jennings Bryan stated at that time,

> The majority is not trying to establish a religion or to teach it—it is trying to protect itself from the effort of an insolent minority to force irreligion upon the children under the guise of teaching science. What right has a little irresponsible oligarchy of self-styled intellectuals to demand control of the schools of the United States?[2]

In 1920, Bryan did not object to the teaching of evolution as a theory; however, he objected to it being taught as fact. He objected to the idea that a few people who actually believed that theory were forcing their belief on the rest of society. Since that time, many small groups with a special complaint or interest have been able to influence our entire system of education. I believe that the majority of our people still have good moral principles. However, we will never again have good discipline and control in our schools until that majority is willing to stand up and change the system. There are some reasons that the minority has gained so much power.

FEAR OF LAWSUITS

When I was in school, there was a simple rule at our house: If you are in trouble at school, you are in more trouble at home. There was no double message in that rule. The message was simple: You must respect authority even if the authority makes a mistake. Believe me, I was never worried about a paddling at school, but I was sure afraid of the belt my Dad had at home. It was that respect for my father's discipline that kept this boy out of trouble.

Today our young people are receiving one of those deadly double messages: "Respect authority, but if you get into trouble, your parents will support you, because after all, you are in the

---

[2]Peter Jennings and Todd Brewster, *In Search of America* (New York: Hyperion Books, 2002), 34.

right—the school made a mistake." As that model of parenting develops, young people become capable of using the system to the point that parents are ready to make the school pay. We are a society that loves lawsuits. Schools are continually feeling the impact of possible lawsuits. Administrators and teachers are afraid to provide punishment because they will be forced to defend their actions in court.

This problem becomes even greater in areas of the teaching of moral values. A few families whose values differ from the rest of the community's are always ready to force the school to accept their values, even when they do not fit with the community's. For example, the American Civil Liberties Union, in cooperation with the National Center for Lesbian Rights, won a major victory January 6, 2004, when they won a $1.1 million settlement against the Morgan Hill Independent School District, in California. The settlement resulted from perceived harassment of homosexual students. As a result of the settlement, beginning in the 2004–2005 school year, all students from the seventh grade up will be forced to take "anti-gay harassment" training. The protection for "gender identity" also prohibits school officials from banning male students from attending school wearing the apparel of the opposite sex. Regardless of the concerns of parents about the approval of the homosexual lifestyle, they will be forced to have their children attend these classes.

The ACLU has used this case to say, "We hope that the outcome of this case will make suing other school districts less necessary." In other words, they are ready to force other school districts to comply with their plan for the homosexual agenda. Before your fears take over, let me assure you we will deal with the solution to the lawsuit issue in a few pages as we address the development of a "moral school environment."

INAPPROPRIATE SOLUTIONS FOR THE PROBLEM OF HARASSMENT

The problem of bullying or harassment is real in our schools. However, while the ACLU would like us to believe that all of that harassment is only associated with gay students, the truth is that many different types of students are bullied. *All* harassment is wrong, whether it is directed toward a nerd or a slow student or a particular ethnic group. So the question arises, How do we address this problem?

There are at least two possible explanations. We can take the approach of the ACLU and decide to defend homosexual students as we ignore the problem with other students, or we can address the problem from an approach of character development. When young people are taught proper moral attitudes, bullying will disappear. Let's look at both solutions and examine the results.

Whenever a school policy is developed, it automatically sends two types of messages to the students: direct messages, which are obvious to everyone, and backdoor messages, which are a reflection of the policy when it is applied to the students' thought processes. When we look at the ACLU's solution to harassment there are at least two direct messages:

1. Harassment is wrong.
2. Homosexuals are an especially good group of people and should be specifically protected.

The more dangerous messages are the backdoor messages, which are not spelled out by the policy, but will always come across loud and clear to the students:

1. "Sexual activity at an early age is good and acceptable for all students." After all, the school is defending these students for their declared sexual orientation, which implies activity. Since this is an unusual form of sexual activity, it also automatically sends the message than *any and all forms* of sexual gratification are acceptable.
2. "Contrary to all the evidence, homosexuality is a good, worthwhile, safe lifestyle." This message comes across to students as the school defends homosexuality in spite of the fact that a 1999 study by the Medical Institute for Sexual Health reported that

"Homosexual men are at significantly increased risk of HIV/AIDS, hepatitis and cancer, gonorrhea and gastrointestinal infections as a result of their sexual practices." Also in October 1999, a study published in the archives of *General Psychiatry* came to the conclusion that homosexual people are at substantially higher risk for some forms of emotional problems, including suicide, major depression, and anxiety disorder.[3]

3. The third backdoor message is, "You cannot trust your parents or your family." The traditional family does not support the homosexual lifestyle, so if the school is defending this form of living, the message that every student will take away from his or her awareness training is that *parents are wrong.* If they are wrong on this issue, there is no need to listen to them on other aspects of life.

4. This message works in conjunction with the third backdoor message: "The Bible is obviously out of date because it condemns homosexual practices." (See Rom. 1:24–27; I Cor. 6:9–11.) This will also lead students to doubt the values of their church and the leaders of the church who teach that such practices are wrong. The whole foundation of their belief system has now been challenged with no one in authority who is able to defend their religious beliefs.

5. "You must make sure that you never stand for anything. If you believe in anything, you may be in opposition to someone else; therefore, you are wrong. Since you must accept homosexuality as a proper lifestyle, doesn't that also mean you must accept any other lifestyle? Living together without marriage—that's got to be okay. Having children out of wedlock—you have to accept that one also. What about the student who takes a stance against democracy and advo-

---

[3]Dale O'Leary, "Recent Studies on Homosexuality and Mental Health," *Archives of General Psychiatry* 56 (October 1999).

cates the overthrow of our country? That has to be acceptable! What about the casual use of drugs? That's just a personal lifestyle choice!"

Do any of those messages represent what you want your children to believe? Don't be surprised when you see a change in their attitude. It's a fact: kids pick up on the backdoor messages!

TEACHING AN ALL-ACCEPTING WORLDVIEW WITHOUT A PROPER FOUNDATION

Can you see the problem? We are trying to expand our children's thinking without giving them a foundation that will allow them to make common sense judgments about right and wrong. Just as you can't do calculus before you learn basic math, you cannot have a strong and useful worldview until you have built a foundation for that view.

Beware of attempts to develop our children's worldview unless they have a solid foundation of moral values to build upon.

We are living in a very small world with a global economy and easy exposure to all the cultures and lifestyles of the world. As the world grows more accessible, we hear the term "worldview" being used more and more. The concept is that our young people need to understand more than just their local culture; they need to understand other people and cultures in our world. It sounds good on paper: A person needs to understand the people with whom he may come into contact during his life.

Before we get too excited about this concept, though, let's remember that we are trying to get elementary and junior high students to understand cultures that are totally different from their own. Can a ten-year-old Christian, American boy from a small town in the South really understand a Muslim extremist who lives in the Middle East and believes that all women are inferior and all Christians are infidels? Can a city girl from a northern city in America really understand a Hindu woman who has never been to school a day in her life?

Can any ten-year-old understand why a person would be so filled with hate that he would become a terrorist with no other goal in life than to destroy innocent people? If you can find some children who can understand those people, have them come explain those lifestyles to me because I have trouble understanding.

We have created a problem by trying to explain the most difficult concepts to children before they have a foundation of knowledge on which to build. Asking children to be accepting of people of all nations and lifestyles is like asking a child to do calculus before he or she can do basic math. We start them with a basic foundation of numbers before we even start with addition and subtraction. Over the course of their education, they build on that foundation until they can understand even the most difficult mathematical problems.

SUMMARY

The challenges we face have developed from three basic problems. First, good, moral people have been backed into a corner because they fear the possibility of a lawsuit if they really stand for the things they believe to be right. Second, inappropriate attempts to stop harassment have been initiated which are directed in such a way that they cause students to accept, without question, lifestyles and ideals that are immoral. As these anti-harassment programs gain strength, they are actually forcing our young people to accept homosexuality and other improper lifestyles. Schools will be much more effective in stopping harassment of all students by building character among students. The third problem is attempts by our schools to direct our students toward an all-accepting worldview before they have a foundation of right and wrong.

STUDY GUIDE: CHAPTER 8
HOW COULD THIS HAPPEN IN OUR SCHOOLS?

I. Discuss the following passages:
   A. Proverbs 9:9–12
      1. How would you define wisdom?
      2. What is the foundation of true wisdom?
   B. Proverbs 10:1
      1. How does a wise child bring joy to parents?
      2. How does a foolish child bring grief to parents?
   C. Proverbs 4:1–9
      1. How do children gain wisdom?
      2. Can there be true wisdom without the Word of God? Why or why not?

II. Discuss the problems that are associated with our current schools.
   A. Why do you think the severity of problems in schools has escalated so much from 1940 to the present?
   B. Do you agree with the author's statement that intellectuals have taken the control of our schools out of the hands of the local community? Why or why not?
   C. What was your impression as you read about the lawsuit against the Morgan Hill school district?
      1. What cases do you know of that involve lawsuits against school systems? In your opinion were those lawsuits justified?
      2. What messages do you think people learned from those lawsuits?
   D. In what areas have you seen teaching concerning tolerance done in an appropriate way?
   E. In what areas have you seen this teaching done in an inappropriate manner?
   F. Discuss the backdoor messages that students receive when tolerance is taught in an inappropriate manner.
   G. Discuss each of the backdoor messages suggested by the author.

III. Discuss the value of teaching tolerance in a proper manner.
   A. What is the direct message of proper moral teaching in school?
   B. Discuss the backdoor messages that are implied by proper teaching on relationships and tolerance.
   C. Discuss the importance of each of those lessons.

9
Dynamic Character Development In Our Schools

A solid local view becomes a foundation for a realistic worldview!

In order to reclaim discipline and character development in our schools, we must look at four distinct changes. First, character development in our schools must be centered around the values of the local people. Only when young people have a good local view will they be able to develop a reasonable worldview. Second, to accomplish this goal, Christian people must develop a relationship with the school administration and teachers. The third essential element is the rebuilding of masculinity in our young boys. God created men and women differently, and our schools should recognize and encourage their differences. The fourth component is placing a high value on the femininity of our young girls. We must develop the strengths of both sexes rather than force them to emulate each other.

DEVELOP A LOCAL VIEW AS A FOUNDATION FOR A WORLDVIEW

In the previous chapter, we looked at an anti-harassment program designed to protect homosexual students. Let's look at the other option to stop harassment in schools. When a school develops an effective "character development" program based on good moral principles, there will also be some upfront messages and several backdoor messages. The upfront message is that good, moral people do not mistreat others. It is morally wrong to bully or hurt anyone. This message is good for anyone, regardless of his or her lifestyle or religion. There are also some powerful backdoor messages your kids will get:

1. "Christianity is an accepted part of our culture, and you can be a good Christian at this school." Whenever good character is stressed in our schools, we are supporting the same values taught by our churches. Both the school and the parents are working to build strong, good citizens. This does not mean the school is promoting religion; it is just helping to develop good citizens. Your children will understand that good citizenship goes hand in hand with their faith in God.

2. "You can trust the values that your parents and your church have taught you." When young people are taught Christian values, they learn to love and care for other people. A character development program that includes training in how to be kind to other students reinforces the goals of parents in helping their children understand right and wrong. When children understand right and wrong, they will not harass any students. This will result in a strengthening of the family, as parents and students will be in agreement with the goals of the program. It will also result in better relationships between the school and parents because they are working toward the same purpose of developing good citizens.

3. "Good character does not include sexual immorality or sexual impurity." When the school is building character rather than defending a selected group of immoral students, the message comes across to students that purity is part of good character. The schools, churches, and the community all support young people who have established a code of conduct which makes room for moral development and will lead to proper sexual relationships. Parents and schools are able to work together to provide proper sex education without a preconceived idea that they must accept sexual immorality.

4. "You can stand for what you believe without being hateful to people who disagree." There is little meaning in life if a person has no principles that are important to him. When a child forms Christian principles and begins to realize that those principles will produce a good, worthwhile lifestyle, he will want to share those principles with others who may have chosen a self-destroying lifestyle. With love and kindness there can be discussions between groups that disagree with each other.

5. **"Children need a foundation for their lives."** The most dangerous place to live is on the sinking sand of confusion. If a child must always adjust his or her values to those of others, before long he or she won't know what to believe or whom to trust. As a result, lifetime decisions are made by guesswork and chance. However, when character development at school supports the character development at home, students have a foundation of truth upon which to make their life decisions. Decisions can be made with confidence, and life can be lived with purpose.

Which type of harassment prevention do you want for your children? Being proactive in your local PTA or PTO can ensure a proper character development program is in place in your schools. Although these organizations are heavily influenced by national organizations that may have values you cannot support, on the local level you can have a positive impact. Remember, most of your neighbors share the same moral values that you espouse. When someone bravely stands up for right, others will join in support.

The foundation for your child's worldview is a good, strong local view. Now I know that is not a term being used in our society, so let me explain what I have in mind. In the quest to understand our world, a child must begin with a foundation which allows him or her to determine good and evil, right and wrong, moral and immoral, along with other important concepts. They cannot understand the world without a foundation to build upon. Let's reconstruct our worldview by starting with a good local view. A child has a foundation set by parents who teach basic respect for others, good manners, and a belief in God. A church that teaches love for others as well as basic moral standards strengthens that basic foundation. The school strengthens the foundation by teaching concepts of patriotism, obedience to the laws, and being a part of society. When the local view has been established, the child has the foundation to understand people who are evil as well as those who are good, regardless of differences in background or culture. Without the foundation, there is nothing but confusion and difficulties. The concept of acceptance without a basis for understanding produces a naive worldview, which can only be destructive. When our children have a good foundation they will clearly be able to develop a comprehensive and workable worldview.

DEVELOP A PROPER UNDERSTANDING OF THE RELATIONSHIP BETWEEN RELIGION AND SCHOOLS

Many Christian parents have the mistaken idea that all religion must be kept away from school. This idea comes from a misunderstanding of the concept of separation of church and state. Our country was established upon a faith in God. Nothing has taken place in the history of this country that should be understood as discouraging religious faith on the part of students. In a National PTA publication entitled *A Parent's Guide to Religion in the Public Schools,* we learn what our laws on separation of church and state intend and what was not intended.[1]

1. "Public schools may not inculcate nor inhibit religion. They must be places where religion and religious conviction are treated with fairness and respect." Compare that statement with what the Plano, Texas, school board tried to do recently when it refused to allow a student to hand out candy canes during the Christmas season because there was a religious message on them.
2. Schools should respect the right of students to engage in religious activity and discussion. Generally, individual students are free to pray, read the Scriptures, discuss their faith, and invite others to join their particular religious group. Only if a student's behavior is disruptive or coercive should it be prohibited.
3. Students are allowed to pray alone or in groups, as long as the activity is not disruptive and does not infringe upon the rights of others.

---

[1]National PTA, *A Parent's Guide to Religion in the Public Schools.* For more information go to http://www.abcog.org/educ/parguide.htm.

4. Public schools are not allowed to have baccalaureate ceremonies. However, parents, churches, or the community can sponsor a baccalaureate service, and the school can advertise it. If you remember the suggestion of the good-citizen scholarship which was recommended in Chapter 3, a baccalaureate service that is well supported by the community would be a great place to acknowledge the winners of those scholarships.
5. Religious holidays offer opportunities to teach about religion in elementary and secondary schools. Teaching about religious holidays is permissible.
6. Religious clubs are allowed to meet during "non-curriculum-related times." Religious clubs may have access to school facilities and media on the same basis as other student-related clubs.
7. Students have a right to distribute religious literature on public school campuses subject to reasonable time, place, and manner restrictions imposed by the school. This one is really important! Parents are the first and most important moral educators of their children. *Thus public schools should develop character education programs only in close partnership with parents and the community.* Local communities need to work together to identify the core moral and civic virtues that they wish to be taught and modeled in all aspects of school life. In public schools where teachers may neither promote nor discourage religion, the core moral and civic values agreed to in the community may be taught if done so without religious indoctrination. At the same time, core values should not be taught in such a way as to suggest that religious authority is unnecessary or unimportant. Sound character education programs affirm the value of religious and philosophical commitments and avoid any suggestion that morality is simply a matter of individual choice without reference to absolute truth.

RE-ESTABLISH THE VALUE OF THE AMERICAN MALE

Have you noticed? We are losing the strength of our young boys! With the rapid move toward a non-sexist society, we have forgotten that there is a difference between men and women!

Turn on your television! How many intelligent, strong male characters do you see? Every sitcom on TV has inept, weak, spineless men being laughed at as the center of the jokes. Look at the roles on TV. The male is almost never presented as a strong leader. I commented to my wife the other day about the fact that you never see a woman cooking on a television sitcom. It is always the man preparing a meal for the woman. There's nothing wrong with a man preparing a meal, but are we forgetting the leadership and strength that should be possessed by our young men? Do we really want to build our young men into inept, weak men like Ray on "Everyone Loves Raymond"?

God created young men with different emotions than women; they are not better, just different. Since men and women are different (and we enjoy the fact that we are different), why not provide for those differences in our education?

In an article for *Psychology Today*, Hara Estroff Marano notes that men and women are different in more than just physical aspects. The gene pools are different, the brain structures are different, the reactions to stress are different, and the responses to stimuli are different. For example, Marano points out that women's perceptual skills are quick to respond, as they possess what we call *intuition*. On the other hand, men tend to focus on minute details and approach things from a detached rational approach. In other words, women see people and events from the top to the bottom while men view the same events and people from the bottom to the top.[2]

Men and women can also develop tendencies toward differ-

---

[2]Hara Estroff Marano, "The New Sex Scorecard," *Psychology Today* 36 (July-August 2003), 38.

ent problems: Boys are ten times as likely to be autistic as girls, while women are almost twice as likely to suffer from depression as men.[3]

In his best-selling book, *Men Are from Mars, Women Are from Venus,* John Gray outlines differences in men and women from almost every area of life. He includes differences in coping with stress, thinking processes, sexual responses, and communication styles.[4] With all these differences, we need to make sure that our schools are protecting the masculinity of our boys!

VALUE THE FEMININITY OF OUR GIRLS

Considering all these physical and emotional differences, do we really want to go against our girls' natural tendencies and develop aggressive, domineering, unfeeling young ladies? Is the in-your-face, hard, tough woman depicted in modern movies really right for the next generation of wives and mothers?

It is time to stress the beauty and softness of loving, compassionate women. As Gray points out in the first two chapters of his book, women are concerned about people and feelings; and they need and want closeness. Women value relationships, and they are comfortable with helping other people.[5] Let's not take these traits away from our young ladies! "Lady" . . . isn't that a refreshing word?

SUMMARY

With determined effort, directed by the good, moral people of our community, we can change these trends in our educational system. Instead of stepping aside whenever the topic of religion is approached in our schools, people of faith must step up and demand the right to express their views. By standing firm, while respecting the ideas of others, Christian people can

---

[3]Ibid.

[4]John Gray, *Men Are from Mars, Women Are from Venus* (New York: Harper/Collins Publishers, 2001), 11-13.

[5]Ibid.

again see the Bible and religion as a part (not the controlling factor) of our local school systems.

People who live by faith must also be willing to help each school to develop a good understanding of the local values of the community. This local view will become the foundation for character-development programs within the school system. It will also eventually allow students to formulate a workable worldview. Local school systems must be careful to make sure they are not being dominated by outside intellectuals who do not share the values or morals of the local community.

To reclaim our schools, individuals in every community must get involved with the development of our schools' long-term programs. Religious and community leaders must take an active role in learning the proper ways to be involved in school activities. The schools belong to the community, and the moral values and religious beliefs of members of the community are an important part of the school. As individuals help restore the character-building programs in our schools, it is also important to take into account the natural differences between males and females. The sexes are different, not superior or inferior, but different. We should help build schools that honor the masculinity of our boys and the femininity of our girls.

STUDY GUIDE: CHAPTER 9
DYNAMIC CHARACTER DEVELOPMENT IN OUR SCHOOLS

I. Review the material from last week's class.

II. Discuss the following Scriptures:
   A. Proverbs 3:1–6
      1. What is the teaching that will give your children life and prosperity? Why?
      2. Why is it important to win favor with God?
      3. How do our children win favor with God?
      4. What does it mean to acknowledge God in all our ways? Does that include acknowledging God in education?
   B. Psalm 34:1–7
      1. How does the Lord deliver us from our fears?
      2. What does it mean to have a radiant face that is never covered with shame? Is that the life you want for your children?
      3. Discuss some ways that the Lord delivers us from troubles.

III. Discuss the concepts of worldview and local view.

IV. Why is it hard for an elementary school student to develop a reasonable worldview? Why is it important for him or her first to develop a local view?
   A. What is your local view of the moral standards our children should be taught? (Please discuss your answers, giving reasons for your beliefs.)
      1. Do you believe that sex outside of marriage should be encouraged?
      2. Do you believe that there are actions that are right and other actions that are wrong?
      3. Do you believe that homosexuality is wrong?
      4. Do you believe that all children, regardless of race or

religion, should be given the same opportunity to a good education?
B. Discuss the facts that help children develop a local view. What is the importance of each factor?
C. How does the local view provide a foundation for a good worldview?

V. Discuss the relationship that should be developed between people of faith and our schools.
A. In your opinion, what is the proper relationship between religious people and our schools? Explain your answer.
B. Discuss the seven rights which Christians have in our school systems.
C. What do you think about the statement that schools should only develop character-building programs in close partnership with parents and the community?

VI. Plan for personal action
A. Start working with school and church leaders to develop a character development program for your local schools.
B. Set up a class in your church to encourage bravery, leadership, and strength in young men.
C. Set up a class to teach your girls how to act like ladies.

STEP FIVE:
REBUILDING
THE FOUNDATION

10
WHY ARE WE LIVING ON QUICKSAND?

**Life's problems are complex;
the solutions are simple.**

To build another great generation, America must look at the foundation upon which lives are built. I remember the first home my parents owned. It was a little three-bedroom frame house where our family lived when my father returned from Korea. Dad was extremely proud of the fact that he had been able to buy a house for his family; however, after only a few years, the joy ended. It seems the house had been built on fill-dirt and the foundation was beginning to shift. The cracks in the walls kept getting bigger and bigger, until time, effort, and money were put into digging piers to support the foundation. It is absolutely essential to have a firm foundation for any endeavor, and people in America today have difficulty finding a solid foundation for their lives.

THE FOUNDATION IS ERODED BY THE CONCEPT OF TRUTH BEING RELATIVE

The great thinkers of our time tell us that truth is relative, that what is right for one person may not be right for another. Scholars are referring to our time as a postmodern world, that is, the thinking has gone beyond the reasoning of the modern age. The main characteristic of this postmodern age is the thought that everyone has a different set of values to live by; therefore, we should accept everyone without trying to change his or her basic beliefs.

The problem, which scholars have already begun to realize, is that without any basic truth to believe in, life just doesn't work.

IGNITING THE MORAL COURAGE OF AMERICA

Robert Coles has interviewed countless troubled teenagers. During those interviews he has heard them talk about their friends, their sex lives, and also about their lonely struggles for meaning in life. Most of them believe that they are involved in a lonely struggle for ethical understanding. They want to know right and wrong, but they are convinced that no one understands their struggle or cares about their desire to have meaning in their lives.[1]

Coles recounts the following comments from a teenage girl looking for meaning in her life: "I look at them [her parents] sometimes, and I think: Lord, they're in a sorry way, even if we do have this big house, and this heated swimming pool, and my dad plays golf and wins the trophies, and he goes racing in his sailboat, and he wins the trophies; a lot of the time, he looks just plain down, but no one, not Mom, not even her, can say a word to him, ask him anything." In response, Coles asks her, "If you could talk to your father, what would you ask him?" She responds, "I'd say—hey, Dad, why are you being this way, what for? I mean, what do you believe in? Anything? Nothing? Your job and your hobbies and us, your family? I'd ask him if he thought he'd be living like he does now, back when he was my age? I'd ask him what really counts."[2]

The postmodern approach to life leaves the most important questions unanswered. There is no real meaning to life if you have nothing that you believe in with all your heart. The teenagers interviewed by Coles had huge problems, but remember, *while life's problems are complex, the answers are simple.* Those answers are found in God's inspired Word.

Dr. Allen Bloom gives eye-opening insights into the value of a life based on a solid foundation as opposed to the sinking sand of postmodern relativism. He states,

> My grandparents were ignorant people by our standards, and my grandfather held only lowly jobs. But their home

---

[1] Robert Coles, *The Moral Intelligence of Children* (New York: Random House, 1997), 153.
[2] Ibid., 154.

was spiritually rich because all the things done in it, not only what was specifically ritual, found their origin in the Bible's commandments, and their explanation in the Bible's stories and the commentaries on them, and had their imaginative counterparts in the deeds of the myriad of exemplary heroes. My grandparents found reasons for the existence of their family and the fulfillment of their duties in serious writings, and they interpreted their special suffering with respect to a great and ennobling past.[3]

He continues,

I do not believe that my generation, my cousins who have been educated in the American way, all of whom are M.D.s or Ph.D.s, have any comparable learning. When they talk about heaven and earth, the relations between men and women, parents and children, the human condition, I hear nothing but clichés, superficialities, the material of satire.[4]

THE FOUNDATION IS ERODED BY THE IMPACT OF CULTURE ON RELIGION

An even bigger problem comes from within the religious world. Well-educated theologians today tell us that the truth is changing with culture. If that is the case, where do I really find truth? What can I depend on to support the weight of my life and my decisions?

For example, in the first letter to the Corinthian church, Paul, by the inspiration of God, plainly states that homosexuality is wrong and those who practice it will be lost.

Do you not know that the wicked will not inherit the

---

[3] Allen Bloom, *The Closing of the American Mind* (New York: Simon and Schuster, 1987), 60.
[4] Ibid., 61.

kingdom of God? Do not be deceived: Neither the sexually immoral nor idolaters nor adulterers nor male prostitutes nor homosexual offenders nor thieves nor the greedy nor drunkards nor slanderers nor swindlers will inherit the kingdom of God (I Cor. 6:9, 10).

The theologians are now saying that Paul wrote only to the people of his day. "Today our culture is different, so we must decide for ourselves if these things are wrong in our culture." The problem is, if we shift that part of the foundation, what happens to the rest of the house? Once one part of the foundation has been moved, why not move another? After all, with divorce being readily accepted in our society, surely Jesus was mistaken when He said,

Haven't you read, that at the beginning the Creator made them male and female, and said, For this reason a man will leave his father and mother and be united to his wife, and the two will become one flesh? So they are no longer two but one. Therefore, what God has joined together, let man not separate (Mt. 19:4).

Once the foundation breaks, there is no end to the cracks that will occur in the building. If we were willing to stand on the firm foundation of truth our homes would be totally different; families would be staying together and working out their problems with the faithfulness that we discussed in Chapter 3.

THE ERODING FOUNDATION DESTROYS TRUST IN OUR FAMILIES AND SOCIETY

When there is no foundation of truth how can you trust anyone? How can you know that people you do business with will be honest? How do you know that your family will stay together? Where can you find any security? Security in our nation and in our homes is found in the foundation of truth that supports our lives.

On December 27, 1969, I was really sick; that is an important fact, because that was the day I married Karen. I wasn't just feeling bad; it was the kind of sickness that makes you feel that you are going to die at any moment. As we prepared for the most important ceremony of our lives, I was lying in bed, and my father sat straddling my chest, shaving my face. That's not a happy picture!

As the wedding approached, everyone except Karen was informed that I was sick. While Karen was calmly preparing for our wedding, I was in a back room, lying on the communion table, hoping to live. As the ceremony started, the minister, who was Karen's uncle, grew nervous and couldn't remember Karen's name during the wedding. Following the wedding, I ended up on the floor in the preacher's office, looking up at a group of people who were wondering what in the world should be done.

At that moment a nurse who was a family friend pushed her way through the crowd, looked down at me, and said, "We've got to get him to the hospital." The hospital is not exactly where you want to be on your wedding night! I am one of the few people in the world who did not attend their own wedding receptions!

The story actually gets worse, but you get the picture. With that kind of wedding, is it any wonder that Karen and I got off to a rough start? Trying to adjust to a start like that without a solid foundation could have destroyed some relationships. However, Karen and I both had the foundation of God's Word. We were committed to the fact that God hates divorce. Because of that foundation, I can honestly tell you, I have had thirty-six great years of loving Karen, and marrying her was the best thing that ever happened to me.

I hope you have gotten the point; the *foundation* is what formed our lives. Without the foundation of our Christian faith, our lives would have been vastly different. If you are married to a person who really has the foundation of God's Word, you can love and trust him or her. You can be sure that your relationship will last. Without the foundation, could you trust your relationship?

SUMMARY

Many people are living on quicksand because postmodern philosophy built around a concept of no absolute truth has served to undermine America's foundation for life. If there is no absolute truth, there is no foundation for good judgment. As religious teachers and leaders have changed their concept of truth as culture changes, our foundation for understanding has continued to weaken. If these concepts are true, there is no truth that can be trusted, no teacher is worthy of our trust, no system of law is worth supporting, and there is no standard of integrity. Our society is left without any functional means of teaching our children a clear view of right and wrong.

STUDY GUIDE: CHAPTER 10
WHY ARE WE LIVING ON QUICKSAND?

I. Discuss the following passages:
   A. Psalm 119:105
      1. How does the Bible light the path for our children's feet?
      2. How do our children avoid the snares of the wicked?
      3. How do the teachings of the Bible put joy in our lives?
      4. How long does that joy last?
   B. James 1:21–25
      1. How can we implant the Word of God in the hearts of people?
      2. How does looking into the Word act as a mirror for our hearts?
   C. Hebrews 4:12
      1. How is the Word of God living in your life?
      2. How does it judge the thoughts and attitude of people?

II. Discuss the three factors that are eroding truth in America.
   A. How has the concept that all truth is relative affected the thinking of Americans?
   B. How does this concept erode the foundation of our lives and the lives of our children?
   C. How has our culture changed religion in America?
   D. How do people view the authority of the Bible today?
   E. How does the concept that there is no absolute truth affect our families?

III. A plan for personal action.
   A. On a piece of paper have each member of your family list the concepts which they believe to be absolute truth.
   B. Write down the beliefs in your church that have changed over the past ten or twenty years.
   C. Look in the Bible to see if these changes are biblical or cultural.
   D. Talk with your family about biblical truth and trusting God.

11

THE FOUNDATION: ABSOLUTE TRUTH, COUPLED WITH AMAZING GRACE

> **"Trust in the Lord with all your heart and lean not on your own understanding; in all your ways acknowledge Him; and He will make your paths straight" (Proverbs 3:5, 6).**

There is a strong, eternal foundation for our lives. The grace of a life founded on God's Word can replace the sinking sand of relativism and stop the erosion of our society.

WHY IS THE BIBLE THE RIGHT FOUNDATION?

If the lack of foundation in the postmodern age is hurting our families and our nation, the natural question is, Why do we believe that the Bible offers a foundation that will help? In response to that question, there are three excellent reasons for faith in the Bible. First, we believe in the Bible as a solution to our problems because it allows us to turn our struggles over to God, who is capable of handling all of them. Second, we will notice that God, who is the creator of the universe, inspired the writing of the Bible, presenting it to us as the natural foundation for our lives. Third, we will demonstrate that the truths in the Bible have been proven to produce a successful lifestyle.

1. God is the answer to the problems of our country.
Many of us could identify with Gideon. His problems were just insurmountable! The Israelites had no leadership and no real army, while the Midianites were invading their land with

an army of 132,000 trained men. Gideon was right where most of us would have been, hiding from his enemies and his problems. Suddenly, an angel from God appeared to Gideon in the winepress where he was hiding and said simply, "The Lord is with you, mighty warrior" (Judg. 6:12).

In my mind I can just see the expression on Gideon's face: "'Mighty warrior?' Who is this guy talking to? Surely he's not talking to *me*! I don't like what these Midianites are doing, but I don't want to risk getting involved."

Isn't that just the way you and I think? In fact, Gideon was so sure that he was not a "mighty warrior" that God had to provide him with *several* signs before he was ready to go to war. Finally, he raises an army of 32,000 brave soldiers. Now think about it: Here is a coward with 32,000 men going up against an army of 132,000 *trained* men. Those are 4-to-1 odds—not really too good! Of course God doesn't need 32,000 men, so He tells Gideon to send home all the ones who are afraid. Gideon must have thought, "Whoops, the odds don't look good!" Twenty-two thousand men agree that the odds are too great, so they leave.

Now we have the coward leading an army of 10,000 men against 132,000 trained warriors—that's 13 to 1. This thing is getting out of hand quickly! But God doesn't need 10,000 men, so He does a little test to see how the men will drink water. If the men lapped the water like a dog, they were allowed to stay, but those who drank in a more conventional way were sent home. Only 300 were allowed to stay.

It doesn't look as if it's going to be much of a fight, 300 against 132,000—that's 440 to 1! I wonder how God is going to help Gideon win this battle! Oh, here's a great plan! Now that you have 300 men led by a "great hero" who has been hiding, let's put a lamp in one hand and a trumpet in the other. Can you imagine how ridiculous it looked when Gideon divided his men into three groups and surrounded the Midianite army with 300 men who didn't even have the proper weapons in their hands?

When they blew the trumpets and held up the lights, they shouted, "For the Lord and for Gideon!" The Midianites ran! What a remarkable scene, 132,000 men running from 300 (Judg. 6; 7). And you and I have the nerve to be afraid to stand up for God! God is almighty. He has the solutions to your problems, and He is capable of rebuilding the greatness of our country! Believe in Him! Trust Him! Take some risks for Him! Then watch Him work!

The Bible is filled with stories of impossible victories won by people who trusted in God. In the Book of Esther, one woman saves a whole nation by her faithfulness to God (Esther 4—9). David as a teenager defeats the mighty giant Goliath (I Sam. 17). Hezekiah prays for protection, and God destroys 185,000 enemy soldiers (II Kings 19). Shadrach, Meshach, and Abednego are not burned by the fiery furnace (Dan. 3). Lions do not eat Daniel (Dan. 6). Jesus Christ is raised from the dead to open the door to eternal life (Mt. 28).

Those are just a few examples of God's power. If He can do all these things, doesn't it make sense that He can work in your life? Doesn't it make sense that He can restore the moral courage of our nation?

2. You can trust God as He is revealed in the Bible.

When we begin to talk about the reality of God, two questions sometimes shake our faith. First, "Is there really a God?" Although most people believe in God, many either live as if He doesn't exist, or they just don't understand what it really means to live for God. When non-believers press some Christians about the existence of God, those Christians are unable to respond with evidence to demonstrate their faith.

This is not a book to prove the existence of God; however, to strengthen our foundation, let me give a couple of reasons why it makes sense to believe in God. There are only two possible explanations for the existence of the universe and life on earth: Either it all happened as an accident, or it happened by design. Which one makes logical sense?

At this point, let me introduce you to John Clayton, who is a teacher and geologist by profession. He holds a Master's of Science degree from Indiana University in Education and a Master's of Science degree from Notre Dame University in Geology and Earth Science. He was honored as the Distinguished Physics Teacher for the State of Indiana in 1985 and S.T.A.R.

instructor for the Indiana Department of Public Schools in 1990. In 1991, he was South Bend Community School Corporation High School Teacher of the Year. The most interesting thing about this very impressive man's life is that he was born and reared as an atheist and was actually a part of the group of atheists that made Madelyn Murray O'Hair famous.

When John was in college, he started dating a girl who was a Christian and promised to prove to her that Christianity was false and the Bible was full of errors. He had even decided to write a book he wanted to call *All the Stupidity of the Bible*. However, after reading the entire Bible four times in one year, he was unable to prove even one false idea.

As he continued to apply science, it became even more obvious to Mr. Clayton that this vast universe could never have existed by chance. When one of the leading atheists in the country, who was teaching at Indiana University at the time proved to have no answers for his questions, John was totally convinced that God does exist and the Bible is His Word. On a Wednesday night in February, after almost six years of trying to prove that God didn't exist, John Clayton was born again by being baptized into Christ. Since that time, this noted scientist has traveled throughout the US, teaching seminars, proving the existence of God. You may want to go to his website, www.doesgodexist.com, to learn more.[1]

With that in mind, let's put the discussion on a more tangible level. Go outside, and take a good look at your car. There are only two explanations for the fact that your car exists: Either it was built by design, or it happened by chance. Now your car is not nearly as complex as the universe, but you would never believe that all that metal just happened to fall into place to create your brand new car, complete with the CD player, automatic transmission, air conditioning, sunroof, and seats that adjust to your body, would you? The only thing that makes sense is that a creator built your car! The only thing that makes sense is that a creator designed and built the universe.

---

[1]John Clayton, "Why I Left Atheism" [article on-line]; available from http://www.doesgodexist.com.

ABSOLUTE TRUTH, COUPLED WITH AMAZING GRACE

The second question is, How can we learn about God? Where do we find the reality of God? Americans are looking in new directions to find God and discover the true foundation for their lives. In recent years, there has been a religious transformation in our country, with millions of spiritual seekers crossbreeding orthodox Christian beliefs with Eastern and New Age practices.[2] In recent years, many baby boomers have made an attempt to return to God and the church, only to become confused, as they have tried to find a church that meets their needs.

The background for the confusion is rooted in the breakdown of morality that began in the 1960s. The consequence of this breakdown was a vast change in the way Americans think about truth. The absolutes of the Bible were no longer viewed as the ultimate authority in all matters of life, including family.[3] You will notice that the search is not really for God; it is for a God that fits the individual's already developed, materialist lifestyle.

Gen-Xers, in their attempt to come to God, reject their parents' self-serving view of religion and have turned to entirely *new* value systems to live by. Many of them have attempted to find those values in traditional churches, only to discover that many of those churches have left the values of the Bible and are relying on their own wisdom to define truth.[4] We will demonstrate that individuals, churches, and our nation can find absolute truth in the pages of the Bible. The foundation is totally solid and can be trusted as our avenue to find God and to experience the life He has planned for us.

Josh McDowell has written two excellent volumes entitled *Evidence that Demands a Verdict* and *More Evidence that Demands a Verdict*, providing evidence of the truthfulness of the Bible. In his work and in other volumes, it has been demonstrated that the Bible is truly unique, different than any other book ever written.

Although there any many different proofs that the Bible is

---

[2]George Barna, *The Future of the American Family* (Chicago, Ill,: Moody Press, 1993), 188.
[3]Ibid., 33.
[4]Ibid., 190.

the Word of God, the strongest proof is in the fulfillment of prophecy. Historians are accurately able to date various writings from ancient times, so it is a proven fact that the Old Testament prophets wrote many hundreds of years before the coming of Christ. One example is the prophet Micah, who lived in approximately 740–700 B.C. Although he lived seven hundred years before Christ, in Micah 5:2, he accurately predicted that the Savior would be born in Bethlehem.

Bethlehem is a small town. How in the world could anyone know that seven hundred years later, in that little unimportant town, the *Savior of the world* would be born? If you will, picture in your mind a small town near where you are living, then think about declaring with certainty that seven hundred years from now the future president of the United States will be born in that little town. Honestly, you don't even know if that town will exist, or if the United States will exist, so how could you predict the birth of a great leader? And yet the Bible not only predicts the place of His birth, but also predicts events surrounding His birth, the way He will die, and the events that will surround His death. How can the Bible be accurate in those accounts? There is only one answer! God, the Creator, inspired the book, and He knows what will happen!

When we accept the marvelous truth that the Bible is the inspired Word of God, we have a really solid foundation for life. God is real; He loves us, and He has given us a pattern for successful living. We must resist the temptation to change that pattern to fit our culture because our culture is man-made. If we are to enjoy the blessings of the life God intended for us, we must stand in opposition to those lifestyles and teachings which deny God's will as it is revealed in the Scripture.

3. Absolute truth combined with abundant grace form a solid foundation for life.

The Bible gives us unchanging teaching concerning right and wrong according to the Creator of the Universe. His foundation of absolute truth will never change, and it gives us the wisdom to make the right decisions concerning the direction of our lives. Some will cringe at the word "absolute" in that sentence because "absolutes" are hard to live up to. That's what is so great about our God: He gives us absolute truth as a foundation for our lives, but also extends abundant grace to those who make mistakes. When we make decisions based on His absolute truth, He blesses our lives; when we fail to live by those truths, we suffer the consequences. Even as we suffer the consequences, we can be sure that He is ready and able to pick us up.

The people who build the next great generation will need a foundation of truth. If everyone is right and no one is wrong, there is chaos. As we have already seen, many young people are reared without the confidence that their lives have meaning. The only real background they have for making important decisions in their lives is their own experience. Why shouldn't they have sex before they are married? Why not be involved in a homosexual relationship? Why not view pornography or sexually abuse young children? Why not get drunk or use drugs? Why not tell a lie when it is convenient? Why should they be faithful to their mates or be involved in rearing their children?

The classic answer is because their parents taught them about those things; however, that is just their parents' reality—there is no reason for them to agree with that reality. Times are changing, and after all, they reason, the whole meaning of life is to find happiness. Because we have lost our foundation of truth, these are the attitudes developing in our young people.

It's time to put a rock-solid, unchanging foundation under our lives and the lives of our children. Why are the above mentioned things wrong? Because God tells us in His *unchanging Word* that sin will destroy our lives. Why should we be concerned about truth, kindness, love, responsibility, and integrity? Because it is the foundation of God's Word that gives us the concepts we use to build our lives. Let's just briefly look at one passage of Scripture.

> The acts of the sinful nature are obvious: sexual immorality, impurity and debauchery; idolatry and witchcraft; hatred, discord, jealousy, fits of rage, selfish ambition, dissensions, factions and envy; drunkenness, orgies, and the like. I warn you, as I did before, that those who live like this will not inherit the kingdom of God. But the

fruit of the Spirit is love, joy, peace, patience, kindness, goodness, faithfulness, gentleness, and self-control. Against such things there is no law (Gal. 5:19–22).

Let's look at the two patterns of life and see which one will help Americans be successful, happy, productive people. The sinful nature offers quick satisfaction, fun, and pleasure without responsibility. Teenagers start having sex when they are young because, while they haven't learned the responsibilities of relationships, they do understand that it is pleasurable. There is never a thought that they may end up like the three teenage girls I have talked with in the past few months—pregnant with unwanted babies by men who have no intention of sharing responsibility for those children. Plans for college will be more difficult, family relationships are strained, and there is not much fun in changing diapers and listening to a baby cry in the middle of the night. Young people never imagine that there could be a venereal disease associated with that pleasure, but 1 in 4 will develop one.

When those young, inexperienced boys and girls take their first drink of alcohol, they are having a good time with their friends. It's fun to be with your friends, let your hair down, and have a good time. They are not thinking about the 1 in 9 social drinkers who becomes an alcoholic. They have never been to a detox hospital or an AA meeting to see the struggles of people whose lives have been ruined by alcohol. You see, anything that Satan offers may start out as fun, but it will end up in broken relationships and broken lives.

On the other hand, the fruit of the Spirit is developed by discipline, courage, and self-control. The fun level is not very high at first, as there are pleasures that you must either avoid altogether or wait until you are married to enjoy. However, love, joy, and peace just get more and more satisfying as life progresses. Older Christians can look back at their lives without regret and enjoy the blessings of their family and homes.

Which do you want for your family? A life that starts out with lots of fun but ends as a disaster, or a life based on God's eternal truth which requires teaching, discipline, and effort but ends with eternity in heaven? If Americans continue to depend on the relativism of modern thinking, our path will continue downhill. We must be willing to accept the absolute truth of God's Word.

You may be reading this and thinking, "My life is already in chaos; I made the wrong decisions, and now there doesn't seem to be any way out of this terrible situation." That's why the grace of God is so powerful. God loves you, and He is willing to give you a second chance. Let me share with you the life-changing power of Christ. In Chapter 6, I told you how Roger influenced others for Christ, so let's talk about one of those people.

Roger came rushing into my office one day in his usual fashion, not taking time to knock or ask if I was busy. He just rushed in unannounced and gushed, "We need to go to the hospital right now!" "Why?" "You need to meet Charles! He wants to become a Christian." Roger was so insistent that I had no choice, so off to the hospital we went. All the way, he was telling me how he knew that Charles was going to become a Christian.

I was totally shocked when we arrived at the hospital room: When Roger introduced me as his preacher, Charles started cursing. He didn't want to see any —— —— preacher! When a rather portly nurse came into the room, he cursed at her and did everything he could to get her out of the room. When she left in disgust, an attractive nurse came in, and he started making advances toward her mixed with risqué comments.

As I offered to pray for him, he showed absolutely no respect for God and wasn't interested in a prayer that, in his opinion, no one would hear. When we headed for the door to leave, not only was I ready to get out of that room, I was wondering what in the world was wrong with Roger's mind. How could he bring me up here to see this man? As we stepped out of the door, Roger proudly exclaimed, "See, I told you he wants to become a Christian!" "Roger, are you sure?" was my reply. Without missing a step he responded, "Of course, I'm sure! If anyone ever needed Jesus, it's Charles!"

The next day, I was quietly working at my desk when Roger came crashing in to take me back to the hospital to see Charles. Although this was not my idea of fun, I really couldn't refuse, so we repeated the scene from the day before. Since Roger is not one who gives up easily, we continued to repeat this routine every day. During the visits, I learned that Charles had a brain tumor and the doctors had said he probably wouldn't live. One outstanding neurosurgeon had told him of a new technique for operating on his tumor, and if they were successful, he would have a small chance to survive the surgery.

The day of the surgery we were in Charles' room as they prepared him for surgery, so I again offered to pray for him. This time he agreed that a prayer would be a good thing. When I finished the prayer, I realized that I had made a mistake by wearing a tie that day! Charles reached up, grabbed my tie and pulled me down nose-to-nose with him. He looked me straight in the eye and said, "Preacher, if I live through this, we've got to talk."

He did survive the surgery, and, about a month later, I met him at his home for a Bible study. Since the first three chapters of Romans deal with sin and since that was obviously what Charles knew the most about, I decided to start the study in the Book of Romans. When I read the first few verses, he remarked in a rather sharp voice, "Who wrote that?"

"Paul did," I responded.

"Read somewhere else. I don't like Paul," Charles remarked. However, after a few weeks of Bible study, this very hateful, mean, sinful man confessed his sins, repented of them, and was baptized into Christ. He had come into contact with the saving grace of God.

> Therefore let all Israel be assured of this: God has made this Jesus, whom you crucified, both Lord and Christ. When the people heard this, they were cut to the heart and said to Peter and the other apostles, "Brothers, what shall we do?" Peter replied, "Repent and be baptized, everyone of you, in the name of Jesus Christ for the forgiveness of your sins. And you will receive the gift of the Holy Spirit" (Acts 2:36–38).

Charles was completely changed by the grace of God! He is

now a faithful Christian with a wonderful attitude about life, and I think he even likes the apostle Paul now! What does his story have to do with our foundation for life? People are afraid of absolute truth because we are not perfect and it is hard to live up to the standard God has set for us. That's why the foundation is so unique: What we are not able to accomplish on our own, the grace of God provides for us. People who have fallen short of God's standard would get depressed and discouraged if God were not a God who provides a second chance.

SUMMARY

The foundation for life is found in the absolute truth of the Bible. God's Word has stood the test of time. The Bible can be proven to be factual and unerring as a guide for human existence. The absolute truths in the Bible are presented without hesitation or apology. When we realize that these unchanging truths have been coupled with the awe-inspiring grace of God, the foundation is solid; there is no doubt about the truth of the Bible. When we live up to that standard, our lives fit into God's eternal plan. When we fail to reach that standard, we suffer consequences, but God forgives us of our weaknesses and allows us to be returned to His loving family.

Without the moral guidance of the Bible, life is almost certain to take a downward spiral. While a life without truth or discipline begins with unlimited freedom and fun, it ends with total bondage and no hope for the future. On the other hand, a life of controlled righteousness begins with discipline and builds to a crescendo of blessings provided by a loving God. Those blessings include peace of mind, a happy home, the love of a church family, and eternal life in heaven. That's a good deal! I think I can live with those blessings!

STUDY GUIDE: CHAPTER 11
THE FOUNDATION:
ABSOLUTE TRUTH, COUPLED WITH AMAZING GRACE

I. Discuss the following passages:
   A. John 14:6a: " I am the way and the truth and the life."
      1. Why does Jesus use a singular term when he refers to the truth?
      2. How does the life Christ lived compare with other lifestyles?
   B. II Corinthians 13:5–8
      1. If there is no way to understand truth, how can a person examine himself to see if he is in the faith?
      2. Explain the statement "We cannot do anything against the truth."

II. Discuss the Bible as the foundation for our lives. Does God really have the answer to the struggles and problems of our country?

III. What problems would be solved if we all lived according to His Word? Discuss the topic of "Absolute Truth."
   A. How has most people's view of truth changed in recent years?
   B. Do you personally believe in absolute truth? Why or why not?

IV. Discuss the Bible as the Word of God.
   A. Why do you believe there is a God?
   B. Why do you believe the Bible is the Word of God?

V. Discuss how absolute truth coupled with God's grace provides a foundation for life.
   A. How does God's grace change our lives?
   B. What examples can you give of people who have had their lives changed completely by the grace of God?

VI. Plan for personal action.
   A. Set up a regular time for Bible study and prayer with your family.
   B. Start a serious study of the Book of Philippians. This short book is designed to give Christians confidence and joy.
   C. Become actively involved in the church.

STEP SIX:
ALLOWING GOD
TO EMPOWER YOU

CHAPTER 12
YOU ARE THE ANSWER FOR AMERICA!

**God doesn't call the qualified;
He qualifies the called!**

In 1938, Adolf Hitler was developing his "superior" race of people in Germany, preparing to invade Poland and eventually conquer the world. Since sports was one of the venues used by Hitler to prove the supremacy of the German people, a boxer named Max Schmeling had become a national hero. In 1936, Schmeling had knocked out Joe Louis in the twelfth round of their fight, thus becoming the greatest boxer in the world. In early 1938, Louis won the heavyweight championship; however, he had never defeated Schmeling. Later in 1938, the greatest boxer in the world, representing the "superior" German race, faced the reigning heavyweight champion of the world, who represented America and the free world. It was more than a fight; it was a preview of World War II and a clash of two worldviews. Before the fight, it has been reported that the twenty-four-year-old Louis visited President Franklin D. Roosevelt in the White House. Roosevelt gripped Joe Louis's arm and said, "Joe, we're depending on those muscles for America."

The night before the fight as Germany proudly proclaimed her racial superiority with great fanfare, Louis sat quietly with his friend, sportswriter Jimmy Cannon. When the discussion turned to the fight, Cannon said he believed Louis would knock out the German in the sixth round. Louis, however, said plainly, "No!" He held up one finger, indicating it was only going to go one round. The greatest fight in history lasted only two minutes and four seconds as Louis, fighting for his country and the free world, knocked out Schmeling in the first round. Louis was fighting for more than himself!

IGNITING THE MORAL COURAGE OF AMERICA

Our country needs your faith! We need you to fight for our moral values! You can change the future of our nation. Germany is no longer the enemy; our own godless society is the new great threat to America. You may be thinking, "I'm not the right person; I don't have the ability or the knowledge." If you think you are not adequate, you are exactly like Moses.

You remember in Exodus, when God calls to Moses from the burning bush, Moses has a handful of excuses to prove to God that he is not the right person. First, he simply explains to God that he is a nobody with no reputation, so he's not the right person (Ex. 3:11). When that doesn't work, he pleads ignorance; after all, he doesn't even know God's real name (Ex. 3:13, 14). Since he has no reputation and is ignorant of God's name, surely the people will not believe him when he tells them about God's plan (Ex. 4:1, 2). When Moses is still unable to convince God that he is the wrong man for the job, he reminds God that he is not a good speaker. Surely God can't use a man who cannot speak eloquently (Ex. 4:10) When that doesn't work, Moses just says, "O Lord, please send someone else to do it" (Ex. 4:13). Moses may not have been the right person, but God is the right God. He selected Moses to lead His people.

You may not think you are the right person to impact the moral values of your community, but you are the one God has placed in your town. You are the one who has the burden on your heart. It doesn't matter what you have done in the past or what talents you have, or your age, or your education; it just matters that God can and will use you! You are reading this book because your heart is in the right place; it is not an accident that you have read this far. God has a purpose for you! Paul said to the church at Philippi, "Be confident of this, that he who began a good work in you will carry it on to completion until the day of Christ Jesus" (Phil. 1:6). Go back to Chapter 7, set your goal, fill out a plan of action, and start praying and working. Then you will see what God can do with your life.

Paul also told us that God is "able to do immeasurably more than all we ask or imagine, according to his power that is at work within us" (Eph. 3:20). If you want to see God working in your life there are a few things you must do.

EMPTY YOURSELF

First, if God is to work powerfully in your life, you must let Him replace your weakness with His strength. As you read this, go into your kitchen and fill two glasses with water. When you have filled them to the top, set one glass on your table. Then pour the contents of the other glass into the one that is sitting on the table. If you have actually tried to accomplish that task, you are either now cleaning water off your table, or you are thinking that I'm a little touched in the head for suggesting such a ridiculous action. Everyone knows that you cannot pour a full glass of water into a glass that is already filled.

In the same way, it is impossible for God to fill up your life with His power if you are already filled with your own doubts and fears. If you want to fill your life with God, you must empty yourself first, and then God can work. The Scripture says of Jesus that He "made himself nothing, [other translations say He emptied Himself] taking the very nature of a servant, being made in human likeness. And being found in appearance as a man, he humbled himself and became obedient to death—even death on a cross" (Phil 2:7, 8). To be available for the tasks that God has in mind for us, we must empty ourselves.

HAVE YOUR MIND SET ON GOD'S WILL

The ideas we have discussed in this book are not important because they are things that please us; they are important because they bring this nation closer to God. We are encouraged in the Word of God, "Do not conform any longer to the pattern of this world, but be transformed by the renewing of your mind. Then you will be able to test and approve what God's will is— his good, pleasing and perfect will" (Rom. 12:2).

In the 2004 Olympics, expert marksman Matthew Emmons had a gold medal almost assured as he took aim for his last shot. He was leading by three points. All he needed was an average shot, and he would win. Emmons took careful aim and fired an almost perfect shot, hitting the target close to the bull's-eye. To his dismay, when the target was retrieved, he discovered that he had aimed at the wrong target! He received no gold medal; in fact, he did not receive any medal as he dropped all the way to eighth place. You cannot be successful if you aim at the wrong target.

Have you ever talked to people about what they want out of life? Most young people will tell you they just want to be happy—and that is exactly why they will fail! Happiness is the wrong target; if that is where you are aiming, you will miss by a mile. If you aim at the wrong target, you will never be successful.

In the Sermon on the Mount, Jesus starts with the word "blessed." Although it has a much greater meaning, the Greek word can roughly be translated by the word "happy." If you look at the statements in the beatitudes, you will notice that happiness is not the target; it is the byproduct of hitting the goal. Read them carefully:

> Blessed are the poor in spirit, for theirs is the kingdom of heaven.
> Blessed are those who mourn, for they will be comforted.
> Blessed are the meek, for they will inherit the earth.
> Blessed are those who hunger and thirst for righteousness, for they will be filled.
> Blessed are the merciful, for they will be shown mercy.
> Blessed are the pure in heart, for they will see God.
> Blessed are the peacemakers, for they will be called sons of God.
> Blessed are those who are persecuted because of righteousness, for theirs is the kingdom of heaven (Mt. 5:3–10).

If you look carefully, you will see that the goals are to be poor in spirit, to understand mourning, to become truly meek, to hunger and thirst for righteousness, to show mercy, to have a pure heart, to become a peacemaker, and to accept the fact that you may be persecuted for righteousness. In other words, the *target* is the will of God; when we live by His will, it is God who provides us with satisfaction, peace, and lasting joy in our lives.

Don't ask, "What will make me happy?" Don't ask, "How can I fit in with the worldview of our ever-changing society?" Ask simply, "How can I live according to God's will?"

DRAW A LINE IN THE SAND, AND TAKE A STAND

According to some historical accounts, early in March 1836, Colonel William Barret Travis, the commander of the Alamo which was surrounded by over four thousand Mexican soldiers, took out his sword and drew a line in the sand, asking all who would stay in the Alamo and fight for freedom to step across the line and take a stand for the freedom of Texas. In that one moment, the history of the state of Texas and our whole nation changed. As a result of the courage of the 183 men who stepped across that line, men and women of courage have stood on numerous battlefields and fought for the highest calling of freedom. There is a battle going on for the hearts of the American people. Will you stand and fight?

Consider the moral attack on our children. According to Juliet B. Schor, author of *Born to Buy*, companies have coined a slogan: KAGOY, or Kids Are Getting Older Younger. As a result of that philosophy, Abercrombie & Fitch has produced a line of thong underwear for girls ages ten to sixteen, imprinted with phrases like "wink, wink" and "eye candy."[1] Why would children buy such clothing? They buy it because their parents allow it. The real question is, Why would any parent think such clothing is appropriate for his or her daughter?

If you understand the difference between right and wrong, don't be afraid to tell your children and expect them to live by your standards. Yes, they will challenge you and even get mad occasionally, but they won't ruin their lives before they are old enough to understand what they are doing. Before we allow our children's morals to be destroyed at age ten, shouldn't we draw a line in the sand and fight?

---

[1] Michael Crowley, "No-Strings Sex," *Reader's Digest* (February 2005), 33.

When you have drawn the line in the sand, make sure that it applies to the adults as well. When I was in elementary school, my temper always seemed to control my actions. The other kids knew how to hit my hot button, and they loved to see the fights that would always follow a little well-placed ribbing. After one exceptionally rough fight, my teacher sent a message home to my parents with these words: "Dean is a very nice boy, but he needs to learn how to count to ten before he gets mad." When he read the note, Dad got red in the face, started yelling and punished me very harshly. Is it any wonder I had a temper problem? Why do our children have such moral problems? They look at us as examples.

By the way, I also had the privilege of observing my father change because he desperately wanted to be a good father and a good Christian. My sister, who is ten years younger than I am, doesn't believe Dad ever had a bad temper. I will always love my father for his great example. He drew the line in the sand for himself so that I could step over with him. If you are locked into a sinful life, you can change; and when you do, it will change the future for your entire family.

LET YOUR CHRISTIAN LOVE OVERPOWER THE DECEIT OF CULTURAL ACCEPTANCE

Christian love is the exact opposite of the tolerance defined by our culture. Tolerance, according to the modern definition, means that you must accept without question the lifestyles of other people. What if that lifestyle is destructive or immoral? If two people elect to have sex before they are married, our culture believes that is just their choice. If a person decides to use drugs or get wasted on alcohol, our culture says that it's just their choice. If we are tolerant according to the modern definition, we will not interfere in their lives.

Wait a minute! If their life choices will destroy them physically, emotionally, or spiritually, and we refuse to help them, isn't that the exact opposite of Christian love? Do we not also have a responsibility to others in society who are being hurt by their actions? Should we not try to protect the husbands, wives, and children of people who are alcoholics or drug addicts? Do we not also have a responsibility to protect children from child abusers or terrorists?

When we really understand Christian love, we want to help people who are hurting themselves. Look in John 4, and you find a woman who is caught in the act of adultery. When people are involved in adultery, they hurt their families; they damage their own peace of mind; and they disrupt the family of the people who are having affairs with them. In other words, *everyone* is hurt! Cultural tolerance says, "Accept them. Don't say anything. Just go along with their choices." What about all the people who are being hurt? The harsh religious leaders of the day said, "Stone her!" That certainly would have kept her from continuing in her sin, but it wouldn't have helped anyone who was involved in this terrible situation.

Jesus took a different approach to the woman. First, He took all the pressure off the woman by stooping down to write on the ground. All eyes would have shifted from the woman to Jesus as the accusers tried to figure out what He was doing. Then, Jesus challenged the religious leaders by suggesting that any of them who had never sinned should throw the first stone. He bent down again and wrote on the ground until they had all left. Then He stood up again and looked the woman in the eye and told her simply, "Go, and sin no more."

That, my friends, is real Christian love. Not accepting sin or approving of it, but providing those in sin with the opportunity to change.

REMEMBER THAT YOU ARE NOT ALONE, AND TRUST IN GOD'S POWER

Every year at Christmas time, our family watches *It's a Wonderful Life* with Jimmy Stewart as George Bailey. Of course, you know the story: George doesn't do anything great with his life, so when he comes to the brink of financial ruin, he is ready to commit suicide. A rather unusual angel, Clarence, saves him and lets him view all the good he has done in his life. I love the show because it is so amazing how many lives one person can touch. *You* are just like George Bailey; you will touch hundreds and even thousands of lives during your lifetime. The only question is, Will they be better people because they know you?

What will God do through you?
Will your life make a difference?

God has a knack for using average people to accomplish great things. After all, He used a young orphan girl who was raised by a cousin to save an entire nation. I'm sure you remember the story of Esther. Ordinary people with great courage accomplish God's will. You remember how King Xerxes had become angry with Queen Vashti for disobeying his orders. Although she was probably right in disobeying an inappropriate request, he was the king, and no one refused a direct order from the king! Vashti was banished by the king; she was never to be allowed to enter his presence again. As the king went on his search for another queen, Esther was chosen as one of the candidates for the honor of becoming the new queen. Shortly after Xerxes selected Esther as his queen, one of his advisers, Haman, developed a plot to eliminate the Jews from the land. He successfully tricked Xerxes into issuing a decree which would have all the Jews in his kingdom killed on a designated day.

At that moment, an ordinary orphan girl became a national hero when she bravely requested an audience with the king. Please realize that in those days, if you requested to see the king and were turned down, you would be executed. This law had been passed to keep people from constantly requesting favors from the king. However, with great moral courage, Esther went before the king to request protection for her people. From orphan to national hero: That's what God can make of people with great moral courage! The Book of Esther is a wonderful example of how God uses ordinary people to accomplish His will.

SUMMARY

You are the one who can change the moral climate in our country! To accomplish such a lofty goal, you will need to empty yourself of all your fears and weaknesses, and allow your thoughts to dwell on God and His power. With your mind set on His power, you will be able to see His will for your life and the lives of your family. As you focus on God's will, life's decisions will become easier and more exact. You will be able to understand when to "draw a line in the sand" against the morally disturbing trends that are destroying the lives of our children and changing the fiber of our nation.

Let me repeat the question:
What will God do through you?
Do you have the courage to find out?

As you take your stand against immorality, always remember that our God is the God of love. We are not trying to overpower evil with evil. Rather, we are overpowering evil with the love of God, which stands firmly on His truth. You will be acting with a love that will never allow your family or your community to be destroyed by the wickedness that is being forced upon our nation.

As your moral courage begins to enlighten your family and community, you will meet with resistance. After all, darkness always opposes light. However, you are not fighting with your own power. It is God's almighty strength which allows you to stand with courage and ignite a new moral understanding among your neighbors.

Now is the time to do something meaningful for our Lord and our country! When you have started a valuable project or made an impact in your community, *please* contact me at www.moralcourage.net (email: dean@moralcourage.net), so I can share your ideas with other godly people. The flame you ignite may inspire hundreds or even thousands of other people!

STUDY GUIDE: CHAPTER 12
YOU ARE THE ANSWER FOR AMERICA!

I. Discuss the following passages:
   A. Philippians 2:2–11
      1. How can the concepts presented in verses 2 through 4 make our society better?
      2. How did Jesus humble Himself to help us?
      3. How can you humble yourself to help others?
   B. Philippians 4:13
      1. Do you believe this passage relates to you?
      2. What are you going to accomplish with God's strength?
      3. How will it help other people?

II. Discuss the five keys which will allow us to let God work in our lives.
   A. How do you empty yourself?
   B. What does it mean to have a mind set on God?
   C. Where will you draw a line in the sand to help make society better? Why? What will you accomplish?
   D. Discuss the difference between Christian love and cultural acceptance.
   E. Why is Christian love stronger than cultural acceptance?
   F. In *It's a Wonderful Life*, George Bailey helped many people throughout his life. With God's help, how many lives will you impact?

BIBLIOGRAPHY

Barna, George. *The Future of the American Family.* Chicago, Ill.: Moody Press, 1993.

———. *What Americans Believe.* Chicago, Ill.: Moody Press, 1993.

Barnard, Catherine. *The Long-Term Psychological Effects of Abortion.* Portsmouth, N.H.: Institute for Pregnancy Loss, 1990.

Bennett, William J. "Quantifying America's Decline." *Wall Street Journal,* 15 March 1993.

Bloom, Allen. *The Closing of the American Mind.* New York: Simon & Schuster, 1987.

Branden, Nathan. *The Six Pillars of Self-Esteem.* New York: Bantam Books, 1995.

Carter, Steven. *Integrity.* New York: Harper/Collins Publishers, 1996.

Coles, Robert. *The Moral Intelligence of Children.* New York: Random House, 1997.

Collins, Gary R. *Family Shock.* Wheaton, Ill.: Tyndale House Publisher, 1995.

Coopersmith, S. "Self-Concept Research Implications for Education." Los Angeles, Calif.: American Education Research Association, 6 February 1929.

Covey, Stephen. *The 7 Habits of Highly Effective Families.* New York: Golden Books, 1997.

Crowley, Michael. "No-Strings Sex." *Reader's Digest* (February 2005).

Diffine, D. P. "One Nation Under God." *The Entrepreneur.* A quarterly journal for the Belden Center for Private Enterprise Education, Harding University, Searcy, Ark. (February 2006).

Freund, Kurt, G. Heasman, L. G. Racansky, and G. Clancy. "Pedophilia and Heterosexuality vs. Homosexuality." *Journal of Sex and Marital Therapy* 10 (Fall 1984): 198.

Glenn, Gary. "Family group tells task force: real threat of violence against homosexuals is attack by their own sex partners." *AFA Michigan* (15 March 2001).

Gray, John. *Men Are from Mars, Women Are from Venus.* New York: Harper/Collins Publishers, 2001.

Greene, Don. *Fight Your Fear and Win.* New York: Broadway Books, 2001.

Jennings, Peter, and Todd Brewster. *In Search of America.* New York: Hyperion Books, 2002.

Johnson, Larry, and Bob Phillips. *Absolute Honesty: Building a Corporate Culture that Values Straight Talk and Rewards Integrity.* New York: AMACOM Books, 2003.

Jones, Timothy K., *Nurturing a Child's Soul.* Nashville, Tenn.: Word Publishing, 2000.

Hicks, Rick, and Kathy Hicks. *Boomers, Xers, and Other Strangers.* Wheaton, Ill.: Tyndale House Publishers, 1999.

Island, David and Patrick Letillier. *Men Who Beat the Men Who Love Them.* Binghamton, N.Y.: Haworth Press, 1991.

Lamb, Micheal E. *The Role of the Father in Child Development.* Hoboken, N.J.: John Wiley & Sons, 2004.

BIBLIOGRAPHY

Marano, Hara Estroff. "The New Sex Scorecard." *Psychology Today* 36 (July/August 2003).

Massey, Morris. *The People Puzzle: Understanding Yourself and Others*. Reston, Va.: Reston Publishing Co., 1979.

McDowell, Josh. *The Disconnected Generation*. Nashville, Tenn.: Word Publishing, 2000.

Newman, Katherine S. *Rampage: The Social Roots of School Shootings*. New York: Basic Books, 2004.

O'Leary, Dale. "Recent Studies on Homosexuality and Mental Health." *Archives of General Psychiatry* 56 (October 1999).

Schafersman, Steven D. "Teaching Morals and Values in the Public Schools: A Humanist Perspective" (March, 1991). Article on-line. Available from http://www.freeinquiry.com.

Schooler, Jayne E. *Mom, Dad . . . I'm Pregnant*. Colorado Springs, Colo.: NavPress, 2004.

Speckhard, Anne, and Vincent M. Rue. "Postabortion Syndrome: An emerging public health concern." *Journal of Social Issues*, 48 (Fall 1992): 95-119.

Staub, Robert E. *The Seven Acts of Courage: Bold Leadership for a Wholehearted Life*. Provo, Utah: Executive Excellence, 1999.

Tomeo, Marie E., Donald Templer, Susan Anderson, and Debra Kotler. "Comparative Data of Childhood and Adolescence Molestation in Heterosexual and Homosexual Persons." *Archives of Sexual Behavior* 30 (October 2001), 539.

Wallerstein, Judith S., Julia M. Lewis, and Sandra Blakeslee. *The Unexpected Legacy of Divorce*. New York: Hyperion Books, 2000.

Weigel, George. *The Courage to Be Catholic*. New York: Basic Books, 2002.